BIG BRAIN LITTLE BRAIN

"It's simple and effective, and I highly recommend it to anyone who owns a business—and not just for you, but your entire company!"
—Jack Canfield, #1 *New York Times* bestselling author and cocreator of the *Chicken Soup for the Soul* series and author of *The Success Principles*

"*Big Brain Little Brain* is a leadership, communications, customer service, and self-help book all rolled into one. Kevin presents the concepts in such a practical, understandable way that stays with you—and the stories he shares are unforgettable. It's changed how I interact with others—professionally and personally—in such a positive and impactful way."
—Carrie Brown, communications executive, major entertainment company

"*Big Brain Little Brain* is one of those books I keep on my desk. There are lots of good de-escalation techniques that have helped me stay sane, but sometimes just looking at the book cover when I'm stressed reminds me there's always a calmer path to communication."
—David Moye, journalist

"*Big Brain Little Brain* is a handbook on how to communicate in all aspects of life. As a mediator, I work with litigating parties to help resolve disputes with the use of effective communication skills. McCarney's concepts of Getting to Neutral and The Tone is the Message are spot on and something I implement regularly with the parties in my mediation practice. It helps me assist the parties in their awareness of their own behavior...their attitude and their tone...and how to use untapped skills to reach the other side to achieve lasting resolution in a wide variety of situations. This book teaches us how to use simple techniques to control our response to win positive, Big Brain legacies."

—Gig Kyriacou, mediation/dispute resolution

"The Big Brain Little Brain concept is one that every school in the world should be teaching, and Kevin McCarney's book should be required reading! The ability to recognize your own internal wiring and make calm and success-minded decisions is something that everyone wants, but very few can master unaided. This book is a huge leap forward in developing a mindset that will ultimately benefit the reader for their entire life. I am so grateful to Kevin for bringing his powerful presentation to our school year after year. My students have benefited greatly from his wisdom and the application strategies that bring the concept into reality."

—Brendan Jennings, Music Director,
John Burroughs High School, Burbank, CA

"*Big Brain Little Brain* is an essential read for anyone who wishes to build enduring relationships in their personal and professional lives. If you've ever thought, "I shouldn't have said that," or "I shouldn't have sent that," then this book is for you. Big Brain Little Brain is a simple read that produces transformative results. You can immediately apply the lessons learned in this book to the next email you send, text you receive, or person you talk to."

—Matt Chambers, Ed.D., School Administrator, parent

"*Big Brain Little Brain* was first presented to Monterey High School students and staff during a Career Day. Kevin shared the impetus for writing the book, and students who are or will be looking for jobs perked up to the topics of successful communication, relationships, and making the most of everything you do. The staff chose to use this book as an all-school read, developing questions and discussion topics to follow each chapter. The book was also shared with parents. It became a common language the staff and students could use to tackle issues. The language is simple—the message has lifelong implications, as we all get stuck in our Little Brain sometimes. I appreciate Kevin's commitment to creating ah-ha moments!"

—Ann Brooks, Principal,
Monterey High School, Burbank, CA

"As a thirty-one-year police veteran with an extensive background in internal affairs, I sincerely believe that *Big Brain Little Brain* should not just be required reading, but a required training process for law enforcement agencies across the country. Day-to-day police work is rife with Little Brain opportunities. Preparing officers for a "reflex" response to avoid Little Brain and stay in Big Brain would significantly reduce the likelihood of physical confrontations. Developing a "reflex" response requires sustained training and evaluation. *Big Brain Little Brain* should absolutely be part of the national conversation regarding rethinking law enforcement training and interactions with the public."

—Eric Rosoff, Lieutenant (Ret),
Burbank Police Department

"*Big Brain Little Brain* is mindfulness made practical and easy. It takes mindfulness out of your head and brings it into every word you speak. In our rapidly changing world, communication is key. The ability to listen with an open heart and foster authentic connection will positively change your life and everyone around you. Kevin McCarney has crafted a simple set of tools combined with powerful principles for building a new world of connectivity and conscious communication. If you're ready to come on board. Now's the time. The world needs you."

—Steven Reich, writer/producer, Hollywood

BIG BRAIN
LITTLE BRAIN

HOW TO CONTROL
WHICH ONE SPEAKS FOR YOU

KEVIN THOMAS McCARNEY

Quantity sales: Special discounts are available on quantity purchases by corporations, associations, and others. For details, contact the "Special Sales Department" at the O'Connell House address below.
Individual sales: O'Connell House publications are available through most bookstores.
Orders by US trade bookstores and wholesalers: Please contact O'Connell House.

 O'Connell House
(818) 840-1177
oconnellhouse.com, info@oconnellhouse.com
verbalintelligence.com

McCarney, Kevin Thomas. *Big Brain Little Brain: How to Control Which One Speaks For You*
Kevin Thomas McCarney. *Big Brain Little Brain Communication Series*
1. Social Psychology. 2. Leadership. 3. Self Improvement. 4. Business Communication. 5. Relationship Communication.
ISBN 978-1-5445-1758-2 (hardcover), ISBN 978-1-5445-1756-8 (paperback), ISBN 978-1-5445-1757-5 (ebook)

Cover Design: Benjamin Holcomb and Scribe (Rachel Brandenburg and Michael Nagin)
Illustrators: Rebecca Butterworth, Eduardo Escalante, Benjamin Holcomb, Richard Shepard, Katelyn Rose, and the team at Scribe (John van der Woude and Anton Khodakovsky)
Layout: John van der Woude
Concept Mentor: Katelyn Rose
Scribe: Natalie Aboudaoud, Cristy Bertini, Rachael Brandenburg, Lisa Caskey, Anton Khodakovsky, Meghan McCracken, Ricky Jump, Will Tyler, John van der Woude, Areil Sutton, and Zoe Ratches

For

*Beatrice Jane, my mother, for being a
lifelong encouragement of personal
responsibility and helping others.*

*Sylvia Miceli, my adopted mother, who spent
many, many years as my business mentor and
showed me how to manage with a heart.*

*Nina, my wife of thirty-two years of love and
support, and our wonderful daughters, Grace and
Katelyn, whose fingerprints are all over this book.*

*Eleanor (Skip) Moye, mother-in-law extraordinaire. She
was a constant beacon of the principles presented here.*

CONTENTS

Good communication costs nothing.
Poor communication can cost everything.

FOREWORD

We are social creatures, constantly communicating with each other in one form or another, eager to let everyone know how we're feeling or what's currently on our minds. So, if what we say reflects who we are, why aren't we more thoughtful with our words?

In a life dedicated to helping others communicate, Kevin McCarney has long grappled with similar questions. Over the years, he has observed how hastily spoken words created unintended consequences. He saw too many relationships damaged because of miscommunication and the long-lasting ripple effect that followed. Often, these moments began with an impulsive comment made under pressure that escalated out of control. He wondered why do we sometimes speak words that we immediately regret, and is there anything we can do about it?

The result is *Big Brain Little Brain*, a powerhouse of practical information that will change your life. It's already changed mine.

Kevin fell in love with food service and hospitality as a teenager, and when it came time for a career, he went straight into the restaurant business. He soon found himself working for big companies in corporate management, where he discovered that training was treated as an event and was all about process, memorization, and tasks, not how to connect with people. But restaurants are more than just food, tables, and chairs. They're about people gathering together for a meal, conversation, and connection.

Kevin followed his heart and created his own place that was about fresh food and personal service with a warm, friendly touch. He got to the core of what restaurants were all about. As he illustrates in presentations, the word "restaurant" comes from the French verb *restaurer*, "to restore or refresh." But in the real world, that is easier said than done. When the time comes to actually restore, refresh, and feed hundreds of hungry people, the pressure is on. And it was in those many high-pressure moments when everything was on the line that Kevin developed a method to train employees and remind himself not only how to remain calm and connected with customers but to make the best of every moment. In doing so, he added his own personal recipe for making the world a better place, one encounter at a time.

But there's more to Kevin than food and hospitality. He's also a dedicated father and a family man. For him, his communication journey really began to take form when he realized he had to learn to communicate with his kids. You don't communicate with kids the same way you do with adults. They require a different level of communication; they require a different tone. Years ago, Kevin wrote a personal essay, "The Tone is the Message," where he fully understood that, "Tone is the primal language humans used to communicate before we learned to craft words." When we are born, our mother begins to communicate through tone much more than words. He observed that the same words in a different tone are a different message.

Kevin's essay was born out of a sincere desire to communicate better with his children, and ultimately with everyone. These early thoughts would eventually evolve into the book you now hold in your hands.

When Kevin asked me a few years ago to help out as a copy editor on a revised edition of what was then titled, *The Secrets of Successful Communication*, I had no idea what kind of journey lay ahead, or even that we would be going on a journey. But during scores of profound conversations, something amazing happened. We found ourselves making stirring discoveries, both universal and personal. It wasn't only the book and title that was transformed. So was I.

Big Brain Little Brain is more than a simple revision of the first edition. It's a complete rethinking of an already perceptive book. It's the result of the countless presentations Kevin has given to high schools, colleges, business groups, and civic leaders about successful communication. As he did more and more presentations, he gathered more and more insight.

And somewhere along the way, Kevin hit on something new. I remember the day we got together, and he told me about the concept of Neutral. It felt like a light bulb had just turned on. There was something missing in the dynamic balance between Big Brain and Little Brain, and that was Neutral. Kevin realized we need somewhere to go, to pause long enough to choose what we say next. The concept is backed up by some amazing people you will meet in this book.

And that's what it's all about. We can all communicate better, but we have to choose to do so. You can read an entire library of books on communication but what really matters is how you respond to the pressure of the moment. When you slip into Neutral, the pressure is off. There's no need to react, stress, or be angry; only to thoughtfully choose what you say next.

This book will help you find your Neutral. It's the key to everything.

On the surface, it may seem like a simple idea, but there's so much more. That's what makes *Big Brain Little Brain* so unique and so incredible. It's a deep dive into anything and everything that enhances or hinders our true communication. It's practical. It's simple. It's easy, and it works. I know, I've been practicing and living it for years. *Big Brain Little Brain* continues to make a positive impact on how I communicate and interact with the world. Even better, if you stumble, there are tools to bring you back. I've used them many times, and every time, I'm a little better for them.

In a world where communication is often more a series of monologues than dialogue, taking the time to listen and be present in the moment is vital. Only through true dialogue can we all evolve and grow.

It's not just what we say that reflects who we are. It's actually how we communicate with others that defines us.

Enjoy the journey.

—Steven Reich, writer/producer

THE TOUR
AND THE EPIPHANY

I grew up in a large, working-class family of seven kids—four older brothers, two younger sisters, and me—in Hollywood in the 1960s. My mother was a hardworking nurse all her life, and my father, although a good man, became well acquainted with bottles of liquor with friendly sounding names (though these bottles were hardly his friends). My father's constant change of jobs kept us moving. Before I was eleven, we had already moved eight times, living in five different houses and three different motels, each with dozens of new people, new places, and new experiences. Long before I learned to read books, I had to learn to read people.

It didn't matter that I was shy. I was on my own at an early age. We all were. New demands were introduced constantly, and I had to learn to handle anything and anyone that came my way. Even as the runt of the litter, I became no one to push around. If you said something, I'd say something back. If you had a strong opinion, I had one, too. If you were snarky, I would try to be snarkier. It was survival of the quickest wit, the fastest on your feet, and the smartest in any situation. In our family, winning the argument became a rite of passage. I did not always win, but I learned never to back down.

This self-preservation instinct came in handy when, at age seventeen, I got a job as doorman at Grauman's Chinese Theatre on the historic Hollywood Walk of Fame. There, my childhood lessons of dealing with tough circumstances were put into practice every day. The theatre's famous forecourt attracted a cast of street characters like bees to honey, and their antics kept me on my toes. From protecting out-of-town visitors being harassed by street characters to handling massive crowds on a nightly basis, I was always dealing with people.

Within a couple of years and eager to move up in the world, I landed what I thought was the perfect job: a tour guide at Universal Studios. Over the course of a few years, I gave hundreds of tours to people from all over the world. I thought I had it made. In fact, what could be better? I was making good money, and all I had to do was deliver the same spiel three to four times a day.

By age nineteen, I thought I knew all I needed to know about how to communicate with people. After all, I was speaking to 400-500 people a day.

Until one day—one tour—challenged everything I knew about myself. It would change the way I communicated forever.

TRAM ON THE RIGHT

It was stifling hot in Hollywood that day with temperatures well over 100°F, and some of the trams (and many of the visitors) were breaking down under the heat. The normal thirty- to forty-five-minute wait turned into three hours or more. While we tour guides waited in the air-conditioned break room, the guests stood outside broiling in the sun.

After several hours of waiting for the few operating trams to return, I finally heard, "Kevin, tram on the right. They're a big group from Europe. They've been in the sun for a long time, and they are not happy. Good luck." It felt like I was being fed to the lions.

As I made my way along the three cars of the tram, I was trying to make eye contact and greet each carload of people—but with little success. They were one large group of arms crossed and brows furrowed.

Approaching my seat at the head of the first car, the leader of the group, who was sitting nearby, grabbed my arm.

"No! You cannot treat us like this. Take us back to our bus immediately and give us our money back. Get your boss over here right now!"

"I'm afraid that's above my pay grade, sir; I'm just a tour guide. But you're going to have to sit down because the tram will be moving soon." My eyes quickly motioned to the driver to get us moving. He did.

"Fine," the group leader said. "I will sit, but we will not enjoy this tour. You cannot make us happy! You cannot make us laugh!" With that, he returned to his seat, surrounded by the other angry guests. His comments got to me.

My reactionary self was upset. I wanted to do something to this group for yelling at me—for putting all their anger on me. After all, I had nothing to do with the heat or the trams breaking down, yet here I was, being disrespected for it. I felt I had a right to get back at them. This, I thought, was just another argument to win. In fact, it would be easy to win by not giving them a good tour. I wouldn't point things out. I wouldn't engage them. They would get what they deserved: the dullest and most lackluster tour possible.

But, as the tram began moving and the breeze began to cool off the passengers, I looked up and noticed in the front row of the second car, a family from the Midwest had been mixed in with this giant group of complainers. They were sitting there, with bright red faces sunburned from waiting the same three hours in the sun like everyone else. I couldn't see it right away, but as I looked closer, I could see this family had smiles on their faces instead of frowns.

Suddenly, my desire to get back at the angry group began to fade away. I couldn't ignore this smiling family. They were so happy the tour had finally begun. They were there for a good time.

I looked at them and decided I would ignore the negative faces surrounding them. I would ignore the comments that had been leveled at me that day and give this family the best tour I could.

Ten minutes into the trek, as the family began to laugh and enjoy themselves, the passengers around them began to lighten up, too. Soon, everyone, with the exception of the group leader, was having a good time. By the end of the tour, there was an unexpected round of applause.

As the large group exited the tram, many people came up to thank me and told me to pay no attention to the leader, "He's always grumpy." Through the thank-yous and good-byes, I also noticed one of my supervisors exiting from the very back row—this tour had actually been a routine audit to see if I was doing a good job. Imagine.

As the group of grateful passengers thinned, I saw that the family from the Midwest had waited to speak to me. The father walked up and said, "Son, you really turned those people around."

I looked at all of them and said, "I could not have done it without you. I was going to give a completely different, not-so-friendly tour until I saw your smiles."

To this day, I can still feel the Midwestern mom's hand as she touched my shoulder and said, "We're so glad you chose to give us that tour. This is the only time we'll ever be in California, and this just made our vacation."

THE EPIPHANY

"You chose." Her words struck a chord in me. They woke me up.

This family, whom I would never see again, had no idea the awareness they had just brought to life in me.

They made me realize that in most situations, I had allowed someone else's words or behavior to choose my own words or reactions. Yet, because of a few smiles on this one tour, I now understood that in doing so, I was giving someone else the power—the power to decide my future, my fate, my reputation. Until that moment, like many of us, I had been reacting my way through life.

That day at Universal Studios was the first time I truly acknowledged that I had a choice—and that the response I chose had an impact not just on my own future but also on that of others.

Because of a few smiles in that moment, I
chose a different response.

This family began my lifetime journey to learn how to make the best of any moment. From that day on, I wanted moments, and their impact, to belong to me.

To the family from the Midwest,

Thank you

"The real art of conversation is not only to say the right thing at the right place but to leave unsaid the wrong thing at the tempting moment."

—Dorothy Fanny Nevill,
English writer and horticulturist

INTRODUCTION

I'm in the people business. So are you. We all are. No matter what you do, or make, or sell, you interact with others every day, building relationships with them. Communication is your biggest asset and your most important export, import, and product. Even if you are not in business, you're always in the people business—with daily communications being your stock-in-trade.

In any relationship, our success or failure is in large part due to our communication skills. Relationships have a very simple measure: if your interactions and communications have left a good impression, people will think and speak highly of you and desire to have you around. If not—if you did or said something that resulted in a negative impression—they may speak poorly of you or be reluctant to support you.

How we handle these moments comes to define us. And in a social world where it can seem like "guilty until proven innocent" is the new norm, and anything you say, text, tweet, or post can go viral in an instant, having control of your words has never been more critical.

THE ROAD TO COMMUNICATION

Most of us gather our communication skills along the trail of life. We're not taught everyday communications skills in school. We acquire them by happenstance from the people around us. We collect them through family, friends, and our experiences—the movies we watch, the songs we listen to, the media we take in. With everyone coming from different environments and absorbing different lessons, this leaves a lot of blind spots and a lot of gaps in our ability to communicate clearly. And in an age when most of our communications are recorded, permanent, and often amplified, we can't let those blind spots blindside us.

Every moment presents an opportunity to react or respond, either to choose our best responses for the day or let our emotions and instant reactions define us. Every communication has the potential for long-term impact on every relationship we have, whether personal or professional. *Big Brain Little Brain* will help add to your existing communication skills, fill in those blind spots, and give you the tools to choose your best responses in every interaction.

> *Every communication has the potential for*
> *long-term impact on every relationship we have.*

DO YOU REACT OR DO YOU RESPOND?

Even though we may know better, sometimes, in the pressure of the moment, we miss the opportunity to say the right thing. Instead, we say things we wish we hadn't. Sometimes, this causes problems.

Sometimes it causes *really big* problems.

Psychologists make a distinction between reacting to situations and responding to them. Reacting happens when you act impulsively, on reflex, without thought. All too often, these reactions happen without truly considering the consequences.

Responding, on the other hand, is taking the time to think things through. In that moment, you realize there's more going on than the single thing someone else just said or did. Here is where you choose how to respond in that particular moment. Making that choice is central to good communication. And a fundamental piece of this book is to give you those "quick access" tools that make it easier to choose a better response.

OBSERVATIONAL STREET PSYCHOLOGY

I have researched and studied communication across hundreds of thousands of encounters with individuals, coworkers, customers, colleagues, board members, and across a world of relationships. There were no lab coats used over the decades, and no animals were part of the study (except our beloved Bella, a rescue terrier, who would sit with me into the wee hours of the morning as I compiled notes, read, researched, and tapped away on the laptop). The bulk of this intensive study took place on the front lines of communications dealing with real-life situations and real people.

The study yielded a pattern to which I've given the name Big Brain vs. Little Brain. These are the two major guiding forces, I discovered, that decide how we react or respond in any particular situation. They impact how our interactions with others advance or diminish and ultimately define our relationships with others.

WHAT YOU'LL DISCOVER IN THIS BOOK

We will distill the complicated into the accessible. You'll discover that every conversation, every encounter, every situation is an opportunity. Every moment holds the space to further your relationships through positive communication or cloud them through poor communication.

Big Brain Little Brain not only identifies many of the common traps of communication we find ourselves in—it will help you navigate these potential communication hazards. You'll find easy-to-remember skills to employ. It offers simple ways to make it easier for you to say the right thing at the right time—naturally.

PART ONE: THE FORCES

In Part One, we'll look at what's going on inside our minds at any given moment. We'll define the main players—the Big Brain and the Little Brain—and look at how they can work for you or against you. You'll discover the difference between the two, where these differences come from, and the Influences impacting our ability to choose between them. We'll break down the parts of a moment—the fundamental unit of communication—and teach you how to approach each beat to create positive interactions.

PART TWO: 7 PRINCIPLES
OF BIG BRAIN COMMUNICATION

In Part Two, we'll unpack the seven principles of communication. Being able to recognize these everyday patterns will improve your ability to control the moment you are in. Each chapter in Part Two lays out tools to help you better navigate these moments. Most importantly, we'll also highlight how to identify some communication traps you may fall into and show you how to spot them and navigate around them with ease.

Let's get started.

PART ONE

THE FORCES

"It's not what happens to you, but how you react to it that matters."

—Epictetus, Greek philosopher

CHAPTER 1

BIG BRAIN
LITTLE BRAIN

hat is happening inside our minds when we communicate?

In my search for why we respond and react the way we do in certain communications, I had the opportunity to ask a physician friend—what drives the differences in behavior between people responding thoughtfully versus reacting impulsively?

Where does this choice come from?

I told my friend that I had been using a story about a guy walking down the street, seemingly normal. One minute he's rational, thoughtful, and in control. The next minute, something minor happens, and he's suddenly disturbed. He's speaking with a different tone of voice, agitated, and appears annoyed to the point of aggravation.

It almost seems like a science-fiction film—like there's a laboratory inside his head, with two scientists fighting over the control panel for his words and behaviors, battling to determine which of the two mindsets will be in control of what he will say or do next.

When the scientist who controls the rational side wins the struggle, the man smiles and says the right thing. People like him; he's happy, successful. Good things seem to follow him when he uses this part of his brain.

But when the scientist in charge of the impulsive side gains control, the man scowls and makes mean, rash, unfriendly statements. Bad things seem to always be in his way, and they seem only to get worse every time he opens his mouth.

"You're not too far off," my friend replied. He simplified the different parts of the brain and their functions for me, sparing me the many complicated technical dissertations on the 100 billion neurons and the 100 trillion synapses in our heads. He pointed me to several books and sources with easy explanations of the main parts of the brain and what they are responsible for.

And what did this science lesson reveal?

Without going into too much scientific speak, the explanation most widely used is that there are three different parts of the brain: the primal reptilian brain, the emotional limbic system, and the two large hemispheres that make up the Neocortex, the big thinking part.

Our reptilian brain is not only concerned with our most primal instincts, fight-or-flight reactions, but also hunger, danger, and the life-sustaining aspects of our body like heart rate, breathing, and balance.

Our limbic system holds our emotions, records memories of our likes and dislikes, and forms conscious and subconscious judgments, which can frequently influence our words and behavior for better or worse.

Finally, the Neocortex is involved in higher functions such as sensory perception, motor commands, and spatial reasoning. It's where language, abstract thought, and imagination come from. This brain is more flexible and aware, particularly in its ability to learn. It's where our "smart" decisions happen.

It's complicated. Further research showed me that there is so much happening in our heads. There are many synapses that connect the different parts of the brain, all firing rapidly and constantly, to assess how we think and feel and react or respond to any given moment. It also showed that the different things going on in our lives have an impact on these connections and our ability to stay focused. Outside Influences—whether emotional, situational, or physical—can impact us internally.

These Influences around us can affect the big thinking brain's ability to override the impulsive reactions of the primal brain. Emotions themselves could fill several books. Here, however, we will focus on how to find a simple way to take control of our reactions and responses to a given situation, no matter what emotions may be at play. Visualize it as the Big (Thinking) Brain and the Little (Primal) Brain battling for control over the emotions of the limbic system. We'll simplify this metaphor and call them simply Big Brain and Little Brain.

In the following chapters, we'll explore the characteristics, actions, words, and behavior of the Little Brain and Big Brain.

We'll look for specific clues to recognize them and learn how to control their power over our communication.

THE CHALLENGE:
BIG BRAIN VS. LITTLE BRAIN

BIG BRAIN

Big Brain makes our more thoughtful decisions and responses. It chooses interactions that make us happy, successful, and well-liked. Clear communication, thoughtful solutions, diffusing a confrontation—they all stem from the Big Brain.

It carefully considers a situation and chooses an intelligent, diplomatic comment or response. It keeps you focused, positive, and out of trouble. Big Brain suggests the words, tones, and facial expressions that convey your best self.

vs.

LITTLE BRAIN

Little Brain, by contrast, speaks to our most primal, selfish concerns and often reacts impulsively. It can't wait to spit out its comment. It doesn't consider what may be appropriate or inappropriate for the moment. It's responsible for many of the "oops" comments that you immediately regret. Little Brain makes the sarcastic or negative comments that may get a laugh in the moment but leave behind hurt feelings and a negative impression.

In our metaphorical understanding of how these two brains work in communication, the Big Brain is much further away from the mouth. The Little Brain is closer to the mouth; it's quicker, ready on impulse. Big Brain's responses, on the other hand, need to travel a longer, more reflective path than the hasty reactions and comments of the Little Brain. Of course, these two "parts" of your brain won't show up on a CAT scan like they do in the illustration. But they will show up in everyday communication.

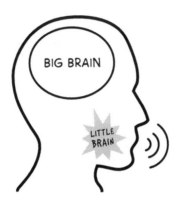

Most of the time during the day, we use our Big Brains as we navigate the different moments we encounter. But there are always opportunities for moments and situations to get the best of us. Something happens, someone gets upset, we feel disrespected, or any one of a thousand other things go wrong. These are the moments when Little Brain is very active and attempts to take over our words, thoughts, and actions. The more aware we are of what impacts our control, the more we can make sure the Big Brain is always in control of our response.

Here are a handful of basic characteristics for spotting the Big Brain or Little Brain:

BIG BRAIN		LITTLE BRAIN
• IN CONTROL		• IMPULSIVE
• GENUINE		• INSINCERE
• STRATEGIC	VS.	• SARCASTIC
• EMPATHETIC		• SNARKY
• THOUGHTFUL		• CARELESS
• KIND		• SELFISH
• GREAT LISTENER		• POOR LISTENER

This is a great place to start your Big Brain journal. Start looking for these characteristics as you go through your day. Take note of how and when they are being used.

"You have the power over your
mind, not outside events."

—Marcus Aurelius, Roman Emperor,
Stoic philosopher,
and author of *Meditations*

CHAPTER 2

UNDER THE
INFLUENCES

hy did I say that? What was I thinking?

Sometimes we say things we regret. More often than not, the cause is something subtle happening in some other area of our lives—Influences we can't see and may not even be aware of in the moment.

In the game of chess, players start by making what's called the First Move. It sets the tone for the game and tells everyone watching which direction you are going. If the first move is yours, it gives you the opportunity to set the course of the game. If the first move is someone else's, you can take control and change direction with your next move.

— BIG BRAIN LITTLE BRAIN —

In communication, your first statement or response is also the most critical because it sets your tone and direction of the exchange to follow.

At this moment—this first move, the first decision—your Little Brain and Big Brain struggle, back and forth, to see which will win control over the next comment made and which direction the moment will take. It's here that the current Influences in your life can make their impact on the response you choose.

YOUR CIRCLE OF INFLUENCES

Influences are all the details of our lives, everything happening around us at any given moment. Influences have the power to affect what you say, what you don't say, and, just as importantly, how you say it. They can pull you toward a Big Brain response or push you into a Little Brain reaction.

In any given moment, you can be under several Influences at once. If positive, they can add to your sense of well-being and calmness. However, Influences can also cause stress and cloud your judgment. While maybe not the same kind of "under the Influence" as we usually encounter, these everyday Influences around us can also impair our ability to keep our Big Brain in control. In fact, not unlike certain substances, a powerful negative Influence can give Little Brain the distinct advantage.

We've taken all these Influences around us every day and divided them into four categories, with two areas in each. These eight slices together make up your Circle of Influences.

Being aware of your Circle of Influences gives you an easy snapshot of how your Big Brain and Little Brain are doing at any given moment. A clear slice (the first image) indicates an

Influence that's in Big Brain mode, and a clouded slice (the second image) indicates an Influence that's in Little Brain mode. Big Brain thinks clearly, while Little Brain can cloud your judgment.

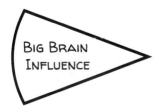

An Influence in Big Brain mode keeps your mind clear.

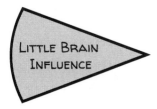

An Influence in Little Brain mode clouds your judgment.

Let's take a closer look at each category and how these Influences can affect you.

PRIMAL INFLUENCES

- **Physical**—This Influence concerns your overall physical comfort. Being hungry or thirsty, too hot or too cold, overly tired, the side effects of medication, feeling ill, or your overall mood will naturally influence how you feel as you approach any given situation.

- **Emotional**—Emotions are among the most powerful of any Influence. We are never experiencing just one emotion; there are dozens of emotions you could be feeling, and you don't need to try to figure out which is one is dominant at this moment. We may not know exactly the right word for how we're feeling, but figuring out which emotions is not as important as recognizing that you or someone else has entered an emotional state. Both positive and negative emotions are deep feelings and can often push us to say or do things we wish we had not.

SURROUNDING INFLUENCES

- **Family**—Family Influences are the most intimate people and places in your life. Spouses, kids, siblings, any of our relatives, and all the things happening in their lives— these Influences impact us greatly. The slice that holds our family will evolve over time as we all grow through life's different stages.

- **Friends**—Whether close friends or acquaintances, old friends or new friends, even friends on social media, these friends can all have an Influence on us. The degree of their Influence can vary with how much they mean to us or how often we interact with them.

CAREER INFLUENCES

- **Work/School**—These Influences involve how we make a living or are studying to make a living. They can involve our relationships with our coworkers or boss, classmates or instructors. They could also be our competition, how the overall marketplace is doing, our grades, or our amount of homework. These Influences concern where we are and where we want to be.

- **Money/Finances**—Money is a constant Influence. Financial obligations, recurring concerns like rent, car payments, or student loans, occasional family obligations, goals for saving for the future, and things like unexpected bills can affect how we respond to all sorts of details throughout the day.

IMMEDIATE INFLUENCES

- **Situation**—Situational Influences result from the current happenings around us or the situation at hand. We might be at a dinner with people who are talking about things that seem trivial. They could be people talking next to us at the movies, the loud volume of music in a restaurant so we can't hear our companion, or sitting in front of a kicking toddler on a plane. Any number of details in the world around us can influence our responses.

- **Time**—Time is another omnipresent Influence. We might be running late for a meeting across town and be stuck in traffic. We want to leave a conversation, and the other person wants to talk more. Time can feel like one of the Influences most outside our control, but Big Brain knows that in being aware of it, you have already put time on your side.

PUTTING THE SLICES TOGETHER

When we put all the pieces together, we get a picture of the total Circle of Influences that can impact our every moment. We can quickly see which Influences may be in Big Brain or Little Brain mode. These Influences surround your core self—we'll call it your Me.

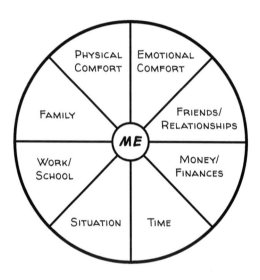

Our Circle of Influences surrounds your Me.

INFLUENCES AND YOU

Some days you may have more than a single Influence in Little Brain mode. When that happens, your ability to keep from blurting out a Little Brain remark depends on the strength of your Big Brain.

Awareness is your Big Brain's greatest tool in fielding Influences moment to moment. Unfortunately, many of us don't pay attention to these Influences and the impact they can have on us. If you're very hungry, for example—and not sufficiently aware of hunger's effect on you at the moment—Little Brain can jump into a reaction or an overreaction before you even realize why.

A strong Big Brain will act as a powerful barrier that won't allow Influences to activate your Little Brain. Even with many of your Influences in Little Brain mode, a strong Big Brain can keep them all in perspective and produce a Big Brain response. Each time your Big Brain can control your response, it strengthens your ability to handle anything with grace under pressure.

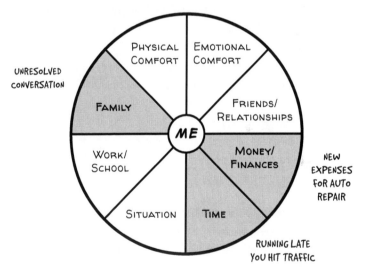

Three Influences in Little Brain Mode.

DAILY AWARENESS CHECKUP

How is your Me today? Does your Big Brain feel strong or weak? Look at your own Circle of Influences and try to identify any that are present or acting on you today. Are there any minor or major Influences affecting you? Are they in Big Brain or Little Brain mode?

Forming a daily habit of self-awareness can help strengthen your understanding of yourself. You'll become more aware of what instigates your Little Brain and what boosts your Big Brain. Soon, you'll also begin to recognize the Influences present in others and why they might be reacting or responding a certain way in a given moment.

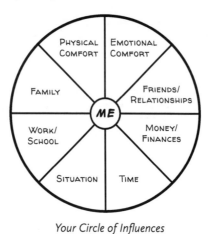

Your Circle of Influences

BIG BRAIN
TAKEAWAY

To help you gain self-awareness, check in with yourself daily to understand which mode each of your Influences is in today. You can even create a little chart like the Daily Awareness Checkup Chart to help you with this.

DAILY AWARENESS CHECKUP CHART

INFLUENCE	BIG BRAIN MODE	LITTLE BRAIN MODE
EMOTIONAL COMFORT	☐	☐
PHYSICAL COMFORT	☐	☐
FAMILY	☐	☐
FRIENDS/RELATIONSHIPS	☐	☐
MONEY/FINANCIAL	☐	☐
WORK/SCHOOL	☐	☐
TIME	☐	☐
SITUATION	☐	☐

"You may not control all of the events that happen to you, but you can decide not to be reduced by them."

—Maya Angelou, American poet, Civil Rights activist, and author

CHAPTER 3

LITTLE BRAIN ACTIVATORS BIG BRAIN BOOSTERS

I n communication, most people default to Big Brain.

Positive things happen and boost our Big Brain all day long, but these moments often go unnoticed and get little attention. We register them and move on because they usually don't seem to have an immediate impact on our day. We will discuss these "Boosters" and their value later in this chapter.

Alternatively, even on your best days when you are fully aware of what our Circle of Influences looks like, there will be moments that catch us off guard—sudden happenings that have the potential to activate our Little Brain.

These in-the-moment surprises can impact us quickly and can give Little Brain an opportunity to jump in and do some damage. These intrusions are "Activators."

You can't always see Activators coming, but they give tremendous power to Little Brain. By identifying them up front, it makes them easier to spot when they do pop up, giving you more control. Recognizing your Activators is the surest way to guarantee that Little Brain does not get a chance to enter the conversation. Let's depict Activators like this:

Ac•tiv•ate /aktəvāt/verb: to make something active or operative

POP-UP ACTIVATORS VS. RECURRING ACTIVATORS

Spontaneous situations that prompt either your good response or your bad reaction are usually driven by an Activator. These Activators might pop up in front of you—out of your control— and seemingly force you to react quickly. Or they may be a recurring problem that you have 100 percent control over solving, containing, managing, or eliminating.

Pop-Up Activators might be someone suddenly swerving into the lane ahead of you or an emergency meeting called by a client on a tight deadline—situations you can't predict, didn't plan for, and don't have control over. But many Activators are simply of our own making. They're situations that occur again and again.

These *Recurring Activators*—which can easily try your patience and make you want to lash out with frustration—are generally manageable and largely preventable. They're the little things that can annoy you to the point where they push your buttons, get under your skin, and set you off. These moments activate our Little Brain and challenge us throughout the day. This is why they're so important to look out for—and resolve.

Among the most powerful Activators are those situations that attack you, your ideas, and your values. We've all been on the receiving end of these kinds of Activators:

- **Comments**: unkind opinions, political bias, sanctimonious preaching, harsh advice
- **Communications**: terse emails, sarcastic replies, vague texts, explosive Facebook posts, bullying
- **Confrontations**: people cutting in line, neighborhood disputes, criticism in meetings

It's one thing to do your best not to be an instigator of these Activators yourself, but what about when they happen to you? How do you handle the mean emails, unwarranted sarcasm, or attacks on your character? With the many tools you'll learn in the pages that follow at your disposal, you'll be able to pause in the moment and respond calmly and impartially.

There are so many petty interactions that can easily activate your Little Brain. Knowing and recognizing the Activators in

AT HOME

POP-UP ACTIVATORS

- Misplacing an important item
- A surprise medical bill
- Plumbing or A/C problem
- Car trouble
- Sudden expense you can't afford
- Surprise storm driving to work

RECURRING ACTIVATORS

- Dishes piled up in the sink
- Inoperable items in need of repair
- Music or TV on too loud
- A fight over what to watch
- Trash not taken out
- Barking, unruly dog

 AT WORK

POP-UP ACTIVATORS

- Being late for a client's presentation
- Sudden deadline from a customer
- Rude customers
- Emergency office meeting
- Coworker taking credit for your idea
- Computer or other system down

RECURRING ACTIVATORS

- Copy machine with no paper
- Air conditioning or heat too high
- Meetings starting late or running late
- Office gossip
- Recurring missed deadlines
- No follow-through on simple requests

 **IN LIFE**

POP-UP ACTIVATORS

- Order arrives wrong at a restaurant
- Long line at the grocery store
- Being late for an important class or test
- Someone swerving into your lane
- Parking ticket
- Rude customer service

RECURRING ACTIVATORS

- Being interrupted
- Someone on their phone while you're talking
- "Reply All" emails
- Waiting for repair company
- Running into "We have a new rule"
- Broken promises

your own life is essential to keeping your Big Brain in control. Whether Pop-Up Activators or Recurring Activators, making your own list can be helpful for getting to know your most common Activators. When writing out your personal list, be mindful of where you leave it. You may not want others to see your notes.

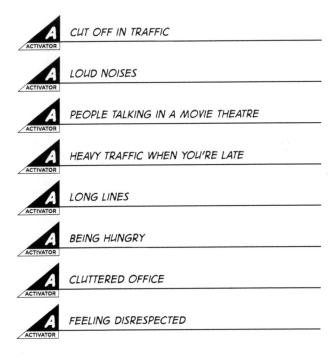

CUT OFF IN TRAFFIC

LOUD NOISES

PEOPLE TALKING IN A MOVIE THEATRE

HEAVY TRAFFIC WHEN YOU'RE LATE

LONG LINES

BEING HUNGRY

CLUTTERED OFFICE

FEELING DISRESPECTED

YOU HAVE A CHOICE

Of course, whether it's a Pop-Up Activator that suddenly appears or a Recurring Activator that you could have prevented, the reality is that once you're activated, you may be vulnerable to a reaction that you might regret a moment later. Regardless of what stirs your Little Brain—though you may feel the need or desire to react—realize that, for a few split seconds, you still have a choice before you do anything.

TERRITORIAL LITTLE BRAIN

Little Brain is naturally territorial and can be easily activated when it thinks its space is at stake. Think of the armrest at the movie theater. Who does it really belong to? What do you do when someone makes an offensive comment about your favorite sports team or TV show? Or worse, steals your parking spot? These moments where you feel the need to defend—or feel you have the right to push back—are most certainly Activators and set up traps that create an opportunity for Little Brain to take control.

> *"He who angers you conquers you."*
> —Elizabeth Kenny, Australian nurse
> and medical maverick

COOKIE D'OH!

Let's look at a moment when an Activator presented itself and how the Influences involved can affect the responses and the overall direction of the moment.

On a very hot day in Greenwich Village, there was a line of more than 100 people waiting to try the newest food craze: raw cookie dough. A group of theater students decided to go together after class. They were about halfway through the line when their friend Julie joined them. A middle-aged man standing with his grown daughter directly behind them said rather loudly, "You can't cut in line. We've been waiting a long time."

Grace, one of the students, gently explained, "Oh, sorry for the confusion. She's just visiting us for a bit, she's not getting anything." The man did not say anything, but his daughter looked at Grace with an apologetic half-smile.

The line continued to move slowly, and the students finally made it inside, where there were still quite a few people in front of them. Ginny, another theater friend, saw on social media that they were there and joined them inside.

The man behind them got upset again. "You are just a bunch of spoiled kids who think you can get away with anything. You can't cut in line." His daughter was truly embarrassed.

The Big Brain Response

What would have made for a favorable ending to this tense situation?

While the group of students were offended and wanted to lash back, Grace again took the lead in a very sincere voice.

"Would you like to go ahead of us, sir? I know we're a big group, and some other friends just got out of class who might be joining us."

The man was stunned and frustrated. He declined and said nothing else. His daughter, on the other hand, spoke to Grace. "That's very nice, but we're fine. We're nearly there. Thank you so much, though."

Both having diffused the situation, Grace and the daughter struck up a conversation and realized they had mutual friends. Within a few minutes, their orders were taken, and Grace and the daughter exchanged contact information.

The Little Brain Reaction

Let's imagine how much worse the outcome might have been if the group had allowed their Little Brain to take over.

When Julie cut in line, the man behind them got upset again. "You are just a bunch of spoiled kids who think you can get away with anything. You can't cut in line." His daughter was embarrassed.

Josh, one of the students, reacted. "Look...just chill out, we were here first." Grace tried to stop him, but it was too late.

The angry man got even more upset. "Entitled brats."

James, another student, looked at the man and said, "It's cookie dough...it's just cookie dough!"

The man's daughter pulled on her father's coat to leave, and he walked away, not quietly, making rude gestures to the group.

Grace and the daughter looked at each other with sad recognition that a simple trip for a snack had played out like this.

INSTIGATORS—DON'T TAKE THE BAIT

Elizabeth Kenny, a self-trained Australian bush nurse, had it right when she said, "He who angers you conquers you." When you get swept up in the emotions of the moment and get activated, it gives others power over your reaction. That is just too much power to give away. Sometimes, others know the things that bother you—what gets to you—and they may try to get a reaction out of you by pushing one of your Activators.

When dealing with instigators, you can approach the Activators they lay out like traps set in front of you. Don't step into them. Don't take the bait. Your Big Brain can refuse to let them activate you. As a result, you know that even if you're on the receiving end of an intentional Little Brain attack, your Big Brain can see beyond the moment and respond in a way that does not allow others to control your reaction. Big Brain will absorb the comment and find the right time and place to distill a response.

Your Big Brain also recognizes that a careless or insensitive comment is not always an affront. It knows that sometimes people blurt out things that may be inappropriate but are not intentional. It can distinguish an "oops" comment from an intentional provocation.

SPEEDING SETS YOU BACK

Nineteenth-century writer and humorist Josh Billings quipped, "The best time to hold your tongue is the time you feel you must say something or bust." He understood the impulses we all have and the need to make sure they do not define us.

Activators are speedy by nature. They speak to Little Brain's natural impulse: fire, ready, aim! When you receive a Little Brain message or provocation from something or someone or find your Little Brain is activated, allowing some time to pass will almost always dissipate its intensity. Time Parachutes (which we'll go into in-depth in Chapter Ten) can help buy you some more time to process and gather a Big Brain response.

BEFORE YOU HIT THE *SEND* BUTTON

Especially in today's digital world, a fast response can seem mandatory. It is not. It's too easy for someone to blurt out a message while activated or to immediately react to a message that activates your Little Brain. When you feel the need to reply right away, remember that in digital communication, whatever you say will be recorded forever. Whether you want to write an impulsive Facebook post about how someone made you feel, send an angry text when you've been stood up, or reply-all to an accusatory, emotional email, pause and take a moment before hitting the Send button.

Think of the last three letters in the word "Send." Once pushed, your ability to take it back or to edit what you wanted to say is over. The end. It will cost you too much time trying to undo and repair issues created by a message sent too quickly. If a communication demands that timely of a response, consider a phone call. Otherwise, it can probably wait until your activated Little Brain is allowed to calm down.

As Lewis Carroll wrote in a not-so-nonsensical line of wisdom in his famous book, *Alice's Adventures in Wonderland*, "The hurrier I go, the behinder I get."

BE PROACTIVE WITH ACTIVATORS

To help you identify your "checklist" of Activators, take out a piece of paper and follow these steps:

1. List the Activators in your life:
   - What are the Activators at home?
   - What are the Activators in the workplace?
   - What are the Activators when you drive?

2. Once identified, look at the list and read it out loud to yourself. Think about how you can minimize the impact or eliminate each of the Activators. Once you break them down, they'll be easier to control.

3. Making just one proactive change today will have an almost immediate effect on your life and your communication skills.

BIG BRAIN JOURNAL

Keep a Big Brain Little Brain journal. Take any bound journal and use the first half for capturing Big Brain observations and moments. Now, take the journal, turn it over, and start from the back to capture Little Brain observations. Take note of when you see Big Brain or Little Brain moments or Activators in play. It could be in a movie, a book, a story on the news, or in your daily interactions. Each week, review the observations. The journal will sharpen your awareness of how to spot Big Brain and Little Brain moments, and it will highlight the consequences of each.

Use your journal to observe your Activators at work and notice any recurring patterns. It will soon become your master list to understanding what may have been at play in different situations and relationships.

You may also want to keep a digital version of your journal handy. You can create two folders on your desktop and place Big Brain examples in one and Little Brain examples in the other. Or you can create two running lists on your phone in your favorite note-taking app. Once a week, review your folders and journal. As they fill up, they'll become a valuable resource to keep close. Keeping Big Brain in focus will help you keep it stronger.

THE GOOD NEWS

Almost any Activator can be turned into a Big Brain Booster with a little effort. You can create Big Brain Boosters easily by doing something for others that is not expected. Your Big Brain will register that effort, and it will leave a lasting Big Brain impression on others. Let's look at how some of the Activators in the different areas of our lives from page 9 could become Boosters:

AT HOME BIG BRAIN BOOSTERS

- Doing the dishes
- Fixing something that's broken
- Letting them pick the show tonight
- Taking out the trash without being asked
- Taking the dog for a walk

AT WORK BIG BRAIN BOOSTERS

- Refilling the copier even if it's not your job
- Offering to get coffee for others who usually get you coffee
- Getting to meetings early and being the first to smile in the room
- Not passing on gossip
- Assisting others in getting their jobs done

CONTINUED...

BIG BRAIN TAKEAWAY (CONTINUED)

IN LIFE BIG BRAIN BOOSTERS

- Ignoring a notification while you are in a conversation
- Going the extra mile in customer service
- Having extra patience at restaurants when food is delayed or wrong
- Being courteous in the parking lot
- Recognizing that traffic sometimes is out of your control

You will soon notice how many booster moments you have in your life. And even better news—Big Brain Boosters are contagious.

BIG BRAIN JOURNAL

Our days hold lots of communication moments—which make for excellent opportunities to observe our Big Brain at work. Notice moments created by others that feed your Big Brain and how they create a positive ripple effect. Take time to think about a situation when someone helped you in a time of need or simply extended an unexpected courtesy. These moments can be easily overlooked, but taking note of them can quickly bring us into a sense of balance as you see how many positive moments are really out there.

- Sarah called to let me know she'll be late
- Someone let me cut in line at the store
- Someone fed my parking meter
- Received an unexpected compliment
- Favorite Barista gave me a big smile
- That guy let me turn first at the stop sign
- Great customer service at lunch
- Neighbor helped me jump my car battery
- Someone held the door for me

Each of these encounters add power to the Big Brain.

"Life is a succession of moments."

—Corita Kent, internationally
acclaimed artist, educator,
and my family's babysitter

CHAPTER 4

THE **MOMENT**

WE LIVE IN MOMENTS

Communication happens in the space of a moment. When you wake up in the morning and greet your family, that's a moment. Each time you use social media, email someone, or answer a call, those are moments. When you get to work, every interaction with your coworkers is a moment. All these moments come together and become the experiences that make up your life, your reputation, and the foundation of your relationships.

Every day will present you with multiple opportunities to create great moments. As you pass people on the street, you'll have the chance to make otherwise insignificant moments matter. A meaningful moment may be helping a cart over a bumpy threshold or letting someone know they dropped something. It might be the way you speak to the barista at your local coffee house or how you engage with a colleague. It could even be smiling at a parking enforcement officer while getting a ticket you know you deserve. Every encounter opens a new moment and new possibilities.

Of course, most moments pass with little or no consequence. But hidden in the middle of those inconsequential moments are the ones that, for better or worse, can shape your life. There are moments behind us and moments in front of us. All these moments connect and add up to your life, your impact, and your Legacy.

MOMENTS OF TRUST

Relationships are built on moments. Far too often in our hectic, overscheduled lives, we simply don't notice the importance of moments as we pass through them. On an average day, we might have twenty or more such moments. Some people could have more than thirty before noon.

Every day, we have conversations with people we've known for years. These conversations provide plenty of opportunities not only to change the direction of these relationships but to clarify misunderstandings and deal with problems as they arise. Most importantly, these moments create opportunities to make the relationships stronger by building trust, one at a time.

Your interactions—your moments—no matter how brief or insignificant they seem, can have far longer-term significance. Even those unimportant moments that occur when you think no one is watching can put you on the road to success. How you respond, how you behave toward others, and the words you use—define you.

When you communicate, what you say and how you say it adds to the trust people have in you—or alerts them not to trust you. Big Brain comments and meaningful moments will leave people with the residual thought that they can trust you. Little Brain comments and moments will destroy that trust.

> *How you respond, how you behave toward*
> *others, and the words you use—define you.*

You will also have conversations with people you've just met. You may feel that you'll never see some of these people again, yet sometimes these seemingly unimportant conversations come back to you and can even turn into vital long-term relationships. What you say in that initial meeting will have an impact. Handle it with care.

YOUR TRUST LEGACY

In every relationship, long-term or short-term, the bond between two people is constantly evolving. The energy is either improving or diminishing. The manner in which the two individuals communicate and act toward each other in any given moment creates either positive or negative energy, trust or distrust—in other words, a Legacy.

Your Legacy is the positive or negative impression your leave behind after the moment. Legacies don't stay in the past, however. We are constantly shaping and confronting them, and they can reappear in front of us at full strength at any given moment. Big Brain legacies will open doors and offer opportunities, whereas Little Brain legacies will place obstacles in front of us to overcome.

Every moment and every choice leaves a trail that collectively becomes your Legacy. It becomes who people believe we are.

ANATOMY OF THE MOMENT

What does a typical moment look like? Someone crosses your path—you see them, you receive a message from them, or you make a call to them. And in that moment, something happens. Whether it's a series of pleasant comments and experiences that increase the power of your Big Brain—or common occurrences that activate your Little Brain—these encounters are the stimuli that begin that moment.

If the stimulus that begins a moment is positive, it will be met with easy acceptance, or may even inspire a Big Brain response, and often leaves you with a pleasant feeling. However, if the stimulus is negative, it can activate the Little Brain, and in the pressure of the moment can cause a reaction, or sometimes an overreaction. Positive or negative, the stimulus is just the beginning of the moment; mid-moment, there is always a choice in how you respond.

You can visualize a moment as having three parts:

- **Open:** You begin the interaction as soon as you engage by exchanging thoughts, comments, facial expressions, and body language.

- **Choice:** As the conversation progresses, you have a choice of Big Brain responses or Little Brain reactions at every beat along the way.
- **Legacy:** Once the moment is over, the Legacy begins. Legacy is how the moment is remembered—it's lasting impression or consequence.

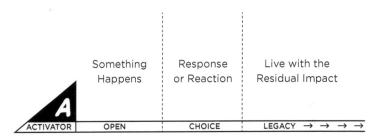

Once the moment opens, you have a choice whether to respond or react—from either your Big Brain or your Little Brain. That choice dictates the long-term Legacy that moment will have.

ARC OF EMOTION

When an Activator appears, there is potential for that moment to produce an Arc of Emotion—an escalation from simple annoyance to aggravation, all the way to anger—in both you and the other person, particularly if either of you are in Little Brain mode. This arc can lead to two very different legacies depending on how you handle it. The good news is that you are in control of whether things escalate—or whether you diffuse the situation and create a calming, favorable conversation.

From the beginning of the encounter, if the other person is in Little Brain mode, they might be activated for just a few seconds (if it's just a minor irritation or annoyance) or for a much longer period (in which case the escalation can quickly become an overreaction). At the high point of the emotion, even logic and facts will not mean much. Their high emotional state needs time to dissipate. Let the moment pass.

THE RIPPLE EFFECT

Inevitably there are those moments that test you, that can, in an instant, take your mild, tranquil day and create a situation where you need to react or respond too quickly. The pressure to act will be powerful. But the ability to read the moment and take that extra bit of time to put your Big Brain in control will not only save you from saying or doing something you'll regret; it will also identify you as someone who is self-assured and composed. When someone is activated, time is the best tool to allow them to come back to Big Brain mode.

You've probably experienced this already. Before Big Brain can get to the point of responding, Little Brain tries to react instantly (sometimes overreacting), often with poorly thought-out words—wanting to vent its feelings and creating a negative Legacy. Unfortunately, this reaction to a moment usually requires Big Brain to do some major clean up afterward.

Big Brain, on the other hand, can—under the same pressure—bypass Little Brain's need to instantly react. It will seek a healthier response, creating a more positive Legacy ripple effect.

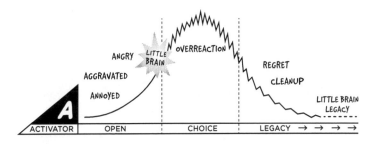

LITTLE BRAIN IN CONTROL
OF THE MOMENT

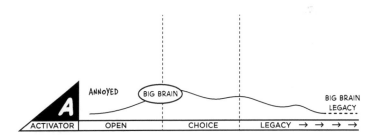

BIG BRAIN IN CONTROL
OF THE MOMENT

WHAT'S INFLUENCING THIS MOMENT?

When a moment opens with the other person in Little Brain mode, think about the Influences that could be driving them. What happened to cause them to open the conversation like that? What is it about their day, their life, or this moment that could be activating their Little Brain? Even if you don't know the answers, if you can stop and consider those questions, then empathize for just a second, your own highly emotional and impulsive Little Brain will not get activated as well. Not only will you automatically begin to see more clearly, but your more rational Big Brain will begin to kick in.

Here's an example of a moment that leaves a Legacy.

PRESSURE OF A DANGEROUS MOMENT

Olivia was finally on the freeway, quickly searching for the next fastest lane. She was on her way to her son's high school graduation, and she was running a bit late. Olivia knew the ceremony was starting soon, and she was eager to get there with enough time to get a good seat. Just a few more exits now, she stayed poised and ready in the right lane.

Alex's morning had turned from bad to worse: today was a big client meeting, and he had overslept, left the house late, and traffic was awful. He weaved in and out of lanes, becoming increasingly angry at every car in front of him, convinced that everyone on the road was working against his need to get to the meeting.

As he neared his exit, he wanted to cut over quickly, but Olivia was in the next lane, right in line with him. Alex tried to cut in front of her, but she felt ambushed by his aggressive driving and didn't want to let him in.

Alex and Olivia's eyes met. Alex gave her a rude hand gesture and laid on the horn.

The Big Brain Response

Olivia took a moment after seeing Alex's gesture. He was obviously in a hurry, irrational, and acting like a jerk. Instead of taking it personally, Olivia slowed down and changed lanes in order to get away from him. She realized that she needed to reset her own time pressure, which would allow her to be a safer driver and get to her destination without incident.

She continued driving and arrived just in time for one of the most important events of her life. As her son crossed the stage, a tear rolled down her cheek.

BIG BRAIN IN CONTROL
OF THE MOMENT

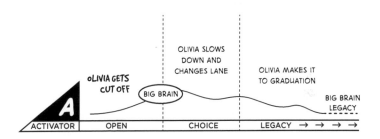

The Little Brain Reaction

The outcome of that moment could have been a lot worse if Little Brain took over.

Olivia, outraged by his rudeness, sped up, preventing Alex from changing lanes. Suddenly the car in front of her stopped-short, and she rear-ended it.

Alex smirked, but the instant he was distracted by Olivia, the car in front of him also stopped-short, and he rear-ended it.

Although they were both just fender benders, the accident negatively impacted the lives of both Alex and Olivia. Alex missed his client meeting and lost a big account. Olivia sat on the side of the road, filling out an accident report. When she realized she would miss her son's graduation, a tear rolled down her cheek.

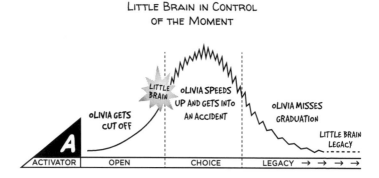

LITTLE BRAIN IN CONTROL
OF THE MOMENT

THE LEGACY OF THE MOMENT

There is a ripple effect to every moment, and that ripple effect lasts long after that moment has ended. Big Brain will always look for ways to end a moment on a positive note, even if disagreements remain. You can almost always find a way to work out problems if you're responding from your Big Brain.

Little Brain, on the other hand, will often end the moment using a negative tone, comment, or snide remark. We all have the occasional Little Brain thought. But it's impossible to succeed in any relationship if you allow your Little Brain to constantly control your encounters with its unfiltered thoughts or comments. It will slowly create an uncomfortable Legacy and discourage people from sticking around to get to know your Big Brain.

It's difficult to always be in Big Brain mode, and sometimes Little Brain will begin to take control of the moment.

Fortunately, even if the moment starts off on the wrong foot, there is a technique to change directions midway through. The next chapter introduces one of our most effective tools and will show how you can, in an instant, take control of any situation and lead it to a Big Brain conclusion.

There is a ripple effect to every moment, and that ripple effect lasts long after that moment has ended.

CREATING YOUR NEXT POSITIVE MOMENT

Our days hold lots of communication moments—which make for excellent opportunities to observe the Open-Choice-Legacy formula in play. However, our days also hold lots of opportunities to experience the Arc of Emotion.

Think about recent moments when you were activated or witnessed someone else being activated. Use the Moment Review Worksheet template below to identify what happened, the response or reaction, and the residual Impact.

Something Happens	Response or Reaction	Live with the Residual Impact

A

| ACTIVATOR | OPEN | CHOICE | LEGACY → → → → |

"Between stimulus and response there is a space. In that space is our power to choose our response. In our response lies our growth and our freedom."

—Viktor E. Frankl, Austrian neurologist, psychiatrist, and Holocaust survivor

CHAPTER 5

FINDING **NEUTRAL**

THE SPACE BETWEEN

I n the years since publishing the first edition of this book, I have given many presentations on Big Brain Little Brain to business groups, city leaders, colleges, high school students, and other organizations. As I conducted these trainings I began to notice that the explanations of Big Brain at play that worked for some groups were entirely different than those that worked best for others. It isn't always easy to find ways to naturally navigate the small gap of time between receiving an impulsive Little Brain reaction and formulating your own Big Brain response. I realized there needed to be a faster way to get to Big Brain, or at least keep Little Brain in check.

We identified the concept of Neutral—the idea of getting to Neutral first before reacting or responding. Neutral is the portal to the Big Brain. It's that little bit of time you take when you recognize there may be Influences at hand—when you might be entering a situation where your Little Brain could be activated. Shifting into Neutral gives you the time to take a quick breath and become more aware in the moment. Once you get to Neutral, you're in control of your response. This quickly became everyone's favorite tool.

After one presentation, I was contacted by someone who had heard me speak about Neutral. He sent the quote at the beginning of this chapter by Austrian neurologist and psychiatrist Viktor Frankl, saying how much Neutral reminded him of something Frankl talked about in his books. I had never heard of Viktor Frankl but was fascinated by the words in the quote.

As I found out more about Viktor Frankl, I discovered an incredible human being. One of the world's greatest leaders on neuropsychology, Frankl focused on a person's ability to withstand tremendous pressure and yet retain a sense of calm and purpose. He wrote thirty-nine books on how humans deal with challenges. After overcoming significant hardship himself—a prisoner of war during World War II, he survived four different concentration camps by exercising his focus on the inevitable (if unknowable) future—he dedicated his life to helping others find their purpose in these difficult moments.

In his influential book, *Man's Search for Meaning*, he illuminates how the mind handled life in the concentration camp, and moreover, how it could withstand such horrors and afterward still apply itself to a productive life.

The space between, what we call Neutral, is the time between something happening to you and your actual response or reaction to it. The space where choices are made. By recognizing that space between, you can slow your impulsive reactions and replace them with your more thoughtful responses. Over time, you can expand that space, little by little, to allow more time to prepare the proper response for any situation. You can strengthen your Neutral like an athlete strengthens his or her body core to be able to withstand great pressure and still perform.

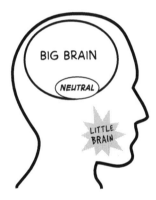

CENTERED

World-famous author Deepak Chopra explains that "The highest levels of performance come to people who are centered, intuitive, creative, and reflective—people who know to see a problem as an opportunity." Being centered is a key component in many disciplines. Their foundations all focus on building up your core and strengthening your center to establish a place of balance. Yoga works on being centered in your body and mind. In dance, you have to be centered and balanced to make the next step. In performing on stage, it is the breath you take before stepping in front of the audience.

In communication, Neutral is centered. It is where choice exists. It is where you can pivot and decide your next step. Neutral is where you know you are in control of the next words out of your mouth, the next expression on your face, the next tone you will use, the next movement you will make. Neutral is the space where you have the freedom to choose. Even if you get knocked off your center once in a while, Neutral will get you back there.

Neutral is how you get centered. It is where you get ready to respond.

AWARENESS

When you're aware of what's going on in the moment, you're able to choose your response. Awareness isn't some kind of unattainable state of mind—it's simply the practice of watching and listening closely. Awareness empowers you to see the moment for what it is and what it can potentially become. Without awareness, you run the risk of blindly following others in your reaction or carelessly following your impulses, even when they're leading you astray. The instant you realize you're activated—the moment you recognize that Little Brain is ready to strike—your awareness can move you into Neutral, and you can be on your way to shifting to a Big Brain response.

WHAT'S YOUR NEUTRAL WORD?

One of the simplest ways to shift into Neutral is to develop your own Neutral Word or phrase that you can say out loud in a non-confrontational tone (or quietly in your head) that will remind you to get to Neutral. It's that first step where you begin to control your response. Your Word or phrase gives you a prompt to help you quickly get to Neutral and find a productive response to the moment before Little Brain has a chance to take over and blurt something out.

Neutral Words can be very common: "Okay." "Well, well." "Interesting." "I see."

Find your own Word or phrase that works best for you and put it to frequent use. Let's look at a few quick examples with a Neutral Word in action. Many of us may already have a Neutral Word but haven't thought about it as a tool.

- After a very long day, you're ready to come home and restore yourself in the peace and quiet of your tranquil house. But instead, you try to walk in, but the door only half opens. Your kids forgot to tell you that they're having a sleepover, and they've decided to build a fort using most of the cushions in the house, right in front of the door. Your first thought is, "What the #@&% is going on?" Instead of saying that, you go into Neutral and say in a calm tone of voice, "Okay..." You greet everyone with a smile and ask, "So, what do we have here?"

- Sitting down to lunch with an important client, you're just beginning your conversation when a group celebrating a birthday sits at a large table next to you. Now you won't be able to hear your client very well. As the celebrating continues, you give yourself a beat out loud, "Hmm." You realize there's a simple fix, and calmly ask your client, "Would you mind if we moved tables? I want to be sure we can hear each other." You quietly request a table away from the party and continue with your client.

- At a conference table, your team is suggesting theme ideas for this year's gala. You spent time researching your idea of "The Three Musketeers," including all the references and props you could use. You suggest your theme and the event organizer immediately responds, "No—it's too similar to last year's Renaissance theme." While you're disheartened by such a quick dismissal after all the work you did (and you're itching to explain why early seventeenth-century France is hardly fifteenth-century Florence), you impartially say, "Alrighty," and then, "I guess I can see that." This gives you space to think about another response. In that time, a colleague has posed the question, "What about Agatha Christie novels?" The organizer replies, "That could work. I like the idea." At that point, she turns to you and thanks you for inspiring the group with a literary theme.

In just a few seconds, your Neutral Word or phrase puts you in control, so you don't need to react. It gives you just enough time for Big Brain to assess the moment and guide you to a more positive resolution.

Below is a list of some examples to help you. Download the Neutral Word graphic from the website—*bigbrainlittlebrain.com*—and write your own Neutral Word or phrase on the Neutral space between the Big Brain and the Little Brain.

NEUTRAL WORD EXAMPLES

- Okay
- I see
- Well then
- Gosh
- Wow
- I had no idea
- Alrighty
- Interesting
- I need time to process this

You can use this illustration as a mnemonic visual to help you get to Neutral quickly before Little Brain can take control.

NEUTRAL CAN PREVENT ESCALATION

What happens if you have every intention of creating a positive moment, but the other person comes at you with their Little Brain firmly activated? Before you even have a chance to open your mouth, the other person is attacking you, criticizing you, challenging you, or doing something they think is funny but offends you, or, if not an actual person confronting you, perhaps an event that's out of your control is suddenly sprung on you.

When attacked in a Little Brain manner, your natural tendency is to counterattack with your own Little Brain. It's simply the body's primal fight-or-flight reaction. But the most productive step to handling anyone in Little Brain mode is not to be pushed into their frame of mind, but rather, to stay in Big Brain yourself.

Your Neutral Word or phrase can buy you time and give you the space you need in these situations. It can prevent the escalation of negative energy from Little Brain and allow an otherwise emotional moment to dissipate. In that short span of time, clear thinking from the Big Brain will come to the rescue.

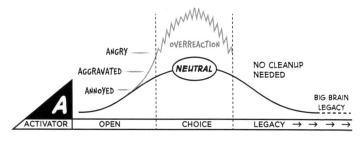

Anatomy of an Activated Moment using Neutral: A negative stimulus creates the potential for escalation, but Neutral takes over and ensures a Big Brain Legacy.

Neutral acts like a quick meditation, an instant dose of calm that shields you from the external stresses or anxieties, and even from the Little Brain reactions bubbling up inside.

CHANGE YOUR ATTITUDE—
CHANGE THE OUTCOME

If there is anyone who knows the power a simple change can do for you, it's Oprah Winfrey. She said, "The greatest discovery of all time is that a person can change his future by merely changing his attitude."

At any point in an encounter, you have the opportunity to change your attitude by switching your tone, using different words, or just becoming more aware of the Influences in that moment. Your day may be going just fine when a sudden event derails your agenda and creates a chain of reactions. Each one of these types of moments gives you an opportunity to adjust your attitude in the moment and jump back into Neutral. When you change your attitude, you will change the outcome—and the Legacy that follows.

THE ENCHILADA STORY

Let's explore an example of customer service communication on a busy afternoon.

Susan and her close friend Linda waited in a long line in the middle of lunchtime at a busy restaurant in West Los Angeles. When they finally reached the counter, Linda ordered a salad, and Susan got a plate of enchiladas. They found a table and began their conversation. A server delivered their meals with a smile.

About five minutes later, Susan returned to the counter and asked to see the manager. He instantly stepped over, and Susan slammed her plate of enchiladas on the counter in front of him, exclaiming, "These enchiladas are cold!" in a voice loud enough for the entire restaurant to hear.

The Big Brain Response

There was a sudden silence as customers looked over. The manager, caught a little off guard, quickly went into Neutral and responded, "My apologies, let me take care of this. I'm so sorry. We'll make you some new ones right away."

Susan returned to her table in a huff, and the other diners returned to their conversations.

Before the new enchiladas left the kitchen, the manager checked to make sure they were at the right temperature. When they arrived at the table, Susan accepted them without comment.

Five minutes later, Susan returned to the counter, scowling, and said just as loudly, "You made these enchiladas cold—again!"

Briefly, the manager thought he might be better off just giving Susan her money back, but instead, he decided to try again to make it right. In a soft tone, he said, "Okay. Let me personally make you a new order. I'll make sure they're hot and bring them over myself."

Susan's anger was still evident as she returned to her friend.

The entire restaurant was watching to see what would happen.

The manager prepared the enchiladas, and they were indeed piping hot when delivered.

"Thanks so much for your patience," he said calmly and with pride. "I guarantee these will meet your satisfaction." Susan accepted them with an indifferent mumble.

The manager returned to the busy lunch rush and almost ten minutes later noticed that the enchiladas had not been touched. Concerned, he approached Susan. He bent low to the table and in a quiet tone said, "Maybe the enchiladas aren't going to work for you today. Let me get you something else on the menu. Whatever you like, it's on me."

Susan was a little surprised. "Fine. Bring me some of those little round taquito things."

The manager got them out quickly and again delivered them personally.

Ten more minutes passed, and the manager again noticed that Susan had barely touched her food. The lunch rush persisted, and he was busy again with a long line of customers. Before he could get over to her table, he felt a hand on his arm. It was Susan. This time, she smiled.

"Thank you."

"You liked the taquitos?"

"Oh, yes," Susan replied. "But thank you for not getting angry at me. I'm really sorry for the way I treated you. I haven't slept or eaten in days. I just came from the hospital, my husband is not doing well, and there's nothing I can do. I just didn't know how to handle it."

The manager took a breath. "I completely understand. Please don't give any thought to us."

Susan sighed. "Thank you again, really. I didn't mean to take it out on you. Thank you."

"I'm very sorry to hear about your husband," the manager said. "Please let me know if there is anything else we can do."

He and Susan traded smiles.

After Susan left the restaurant, several customers approached the manager and complimented him on the way he had handled the moment. They let him know that the way he responded made them feel comfortable, and even more so when they heard her apology. The whole experience made their day. They, along with Susan, continued to be repeat customers for years.

The Little Brain Reaction

Let's take another look. Think back to our Circle of Influences. Susan was tired, hungry, emotionally distraught about her husband, and had just come from the hospital, which had left her feeling fearful. Without realizing it, she used the enchiladas as a way to cope with some of these powerful Influences, and she let those Influences guide her reactions.

Realize the most important lesson of this story: it was never about the enchiladas. Susan's criticisms weren't personal; they were coming from a place that had nothing to do with the food, the service, the manager, or the situation—but rather from other Influences in her life.

Rather than let her actions define the moment, the manager responded from his Big Brain. He didn't take her comments personally and quickly entered Neutral before each response. With other choices or reactions, he might have lost Susan's business permanently, along with some of the other diners. Instead, he let his Big Brain bring the incident to a successful conclusion for everyone: brightening Susan's tough day, creating a moment that encouraged returning customers, and leaving everyone with a lasting impression of great service under pressure.

LITTLE BRAIN BEGINS THE MOMENT, NEUTRAL TAKES OVER

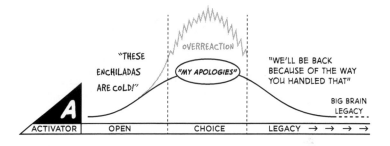

BIG BRAIN
TAKEAWAY

FINDING YOUR NEUTRAL

Your Neutral Word, in the correct tone, can act as a pressure relief valve for the frustrations or anxieties of the moment and begin to dissipate them. It sends a signal to your Big Brain to take over and not to let your Little Brain speak for you. The next few steps will reap great rewards.

1. Jot down a few Neutral phrases you can use for most of these situations, such as:
   - "Okay."
   - "I think I understand."
   - "Got it."
   - "I see."
2. Practice the tone of your Neutral Words. Stay clear of sarcasm, arrogance, or blunt force, as those tones will escalate the situation rather than diffuse it.
3. In a mirror at home, practice your Neutral Word or phrase. Look at your facial expression. Is it also Neutral? Practice every day. Like an athlete training to improve performance, you can strengthen your Neutral to handle any situation.

CONTINUED...

BIG BRAIN TAKEAWAY (CONTINUED)

4. When your chosen Neutral Word or phrase feels and sounds natural for you, take it out for a try.
5. Keep a list of the ones that have the most impact and put them in your smartphone for easy access. For a template you can download, visit *bigbrainlittlebrain.com*.

PART TWO

7 PRINCIPLES OF BIG BRAIN COMMUNICATION

CONTROL
TONE
WORDS
TIME
RESPONSIBILITY
POWER
AWARENESS

"The capacity to learn is a gift;
The ability to learn is a skill;
The willingness to learn is a choice."

—Brian Herbert, *New York Times*
bestselling author

CHAPTER 6

THE **7 PRINCIPLES**

N ow that we know what's going on inside our minds at any given moment—Big Brain and Little Brain constantly battling for control, the Activators or Influences at play, and how moments present us with choices—it's time to see these factors in action. How do we navigate each of these factors in our day-to-day encounters?

More often than not, it's not about the enchiladas of the moment. Unseen and instant Activators can take over even the best of us. Yet, just as in the enchilada story, the impact of our communications can be felt far beyond the moment. Even though the exchange was directly between Susan and the manager, everyone in the restaurant was listening and involved with the resolution. Our everyday interactions leave a powerful Legacy, guided by those in-the-moment choices from our Big Brain or Little Brain. That Legacy ultimately defines our relationships.

In Part Two of this book, we'll look at seven common communication patterns—The 7 Principles—and detail how to approach each of these principles in the moment. Each chapter has three sections. We'll begin each chapter with a story, each inspired by true events, that illustrates the given principle in action. Then we'll look at the elements that make the principle more recognizable. And finally, at the end of each chapter, there are tools you can use to exercise your Big Brain and avoid your Little Brain in each of these encounters.

It is important to note that a person is not Big Brain or Little Brain dominant, but their words and actions can be. As we identify the residual impact of these words and actions, we will highlight a Legacy Word for each tool and trap that speaks to the Legacy the moment leaves and how it will be remembered. Keep in mind there will likely be several active principles in any given conversation, but each principle has its own unique place.

7 DAYS TO BIG BRAIN

The most effective way to get started is to read and internalize one of these seven principles each morning for a week. Then spend the remainder of that day incorporating the Big Brain Tools and avoiding the Little Brain Traps you learned. Journal your observations and experiences each day.

As you begin to understand what goes on within each of us as human beings—and the communication patterns that often play out in our everyday interactions—you'll begin to recognize these Tools and Traps. By the end of the week, navigating these elements of communication will become more and more natural to you, and your Big Brain will be a regular companion.

TOOLS THAT LEAVE A FAVORABLE LEGACY

TOOL

Throughout the following chapters, you'll discover Big Brain Tools you can use in any communication encounter. Remember, Big Brain thinks clearly, allowing you to win the moment. With each of these Tools, we've added a "Legacy Word" and placed it in the Legacy Rewards Card, showing the Legacy you leave when this particular Tool is used.

LEGACY REWARDS

COMPOSED

TRAP

TRAPS To WATCH OUT FoR

We'll also present Little Brain Traps throughout the next several chapters. Like Little Brain Influences, Traps can cloud the moment. With each of these Traps, a "baggage word" has been added that indicates the negative Legacy that follows you when you fall into this particular Trap.

RUDE

AND WE'LL SHOW YOU HOW EACH SOUNDS IN A SPEECH BUBBLE

"If you don't control your
mind, someone else will."

—John Allston,
eighteenth-century author

CHAPTER 7

PRINCIPLE 1:
CONTROL

THE STORY BEGINS:
CHOICE UNDER PRESSURE

E xecutives of the real estate firm MacDougal and Peralta
were getting together to brainstorm ways to accommodate
the needs of a new client. The new client had approached
M&P about representing them on several new develop-
ments they were building. The Executive Vice President, Mr.
Jenkins, in an authoritative tone began to outline the situation
they were facing and advocate his own idea of how to handle
this exciting new business opportunity. The client had several

unique demands, and the meeting was called to discuss how to proceed with them.

After outlining the challenges they were up against and his solution, Mr. Jenkins said, "Well, these are my ideas on how this should go, but I'm willing to listen to anyone else who has some thoughts."

Without hesitation, Tanya, a new associate, jumped at the chance to offer what she believed to be the ideal solution. Full of energy and already proving herself to be an asset to the company, Tanya was quickly gaining a reputation for being intelligent and eager, but not always able to stand up for her own ideas against louder, stronger personalities.

By contrast, the office manager, Finney, had negotiated tough contracts with clients, navigated touchy office politics with ease, and won the respect of his team members. He knew that ultimately he would have to weigh in on the best solution but was reserving his opinion for now.

Partway through listening to Tanya define her solution, Finney's good friend Franklin leaned over and said, "Tanya has a good idea, don't you think?"

"Wait," Finney replied. "We need to hear all of this."

When Tanya was nearly finished, the agents in the room seemed pleased.

Mr. Jenkins, who hadn't really been listening to Tanya, interrupted to tell her why her ideas would not work. He went on to talk about his own ideas again, using his booming, authoritative voice and gesturing in a way that showed he clearly wanted to sway everyone to his line of thinking.

A communication moment—and an opportunity—was created when it became apparent to Finney and everyone else that

Tanya had the better idea. It was well thought out and would certainly solve the client's problem, but it would require more work in the short term. Someone needed to speak up, and it was Finney's responsibility.

There was only one problem: Finney was up for a promotion, and Jenkins played a major part in confirming the promotion... or not.

While he was generally reasonable in his management style, Mr. Jenkins sometimes made his employees feel that choosing something other than his plan was a personal affront, rather than a strategic decision. Siding with him, although his solution was clearly the wrong choice, would increase Finney's chance of that promotion. And while temporarily sidelining Tanya's idea would be the result, she was young with a promising career in front of her. She would have many other opportunities to shine.

Deep in thought, Finney realized the room had fallen silent. That was when it hit him: everyone in the office was looking to him to choose a side.

"Well, Finney. What do you think?" boomed Mr. Jenkins. Finney had a choice.

THE BIG BRAIN RESPONSE

Looking at everyone in the room, Finney explained why Tanya's idea was the clear, strategic choice. He credited her with a long-term vision of what the company could do for this client, as well as the potential this solution created for even more business in the future. He also explained that choosing her plan meant more work for the team now but could make a difference in how the company was perceived in the future. Finney heard the future in Tanya's presentation.

Risking a glance at Jenkins, who seemed taken aback by Finney's honesty, the meeting came to a close with Tanya's plan in place. But Finney's promotion didn't materialize. A few days later, Mr. Jenkins asked Finney to come to his office.

"I understand why you chose Tanya's plan," Mr. Jenkins began. "I know I sometimes dominate the conversation when it comes to solutions. It could not have been easy to disagree with me, but I know I can trust you to speak the truth, even if you and I don't see eye to eye. However, I had to go with someone else for that position based on expertise. It's not personal; I am sure you understand."

Finney left Mr. Jenkins's office disappointed but feeling lighter somehow. Finney's Legacy of respect spread throughout the office, and with his personal integrity intact, he felt emboldened to speak the truth. There would be more opportunities for him.

THE LITTLE BRAIN REACTION

This encounter could have ended quite differently if Finney hadn't chosen to respond in a thoughtful and truthful way. Let's take a look at how a Little Brain reaction might have looked.

Finney looked Mr. Jenkins squarely in the eye and said, "I think your solution is the best way to go."

The energy immediately left the room like air out of a balloon. Deflated and defeated, Tanya looked away, trying to hide her disappointment. Meanwhile, Finney could feel the incredulous eyes of the other associates tunneling into him as he touted Mr. Jenkins' vision and solution as the best one possible.

A few days later, Finney was given the promotion, but it felt empty. No longer excited about the possibility of leading the team he had previously felt connected to, his Legacy was a loss of respect from the people he must now lead.

ELEMENTS OF CONTROL

The story of the real estate firm and Finney's dilemma gives us an idea of how the first principle, control, plays out in everyday work situations. We can respond from our Big Brain or react from our Little Brain. It's always your choice—it's always your Legacy.

BIG EARS, LITTLE EARS

Listening is where control begins. Listening is where connection begins. Listening is where understanding begins.

When you use your ears to truly listen, your Big Brain and Little Brain are both attentive—challenging each other for control of the information. Big Brain listens carefully to everything that is being said in order to completely understand what is being communicated. Big Brain gives the other person its complete attention because it wants to be engaged in the conversation. Big Brain is a master of the art of listening.

Little Brain, on the other hand, filters the message to eliminate anything it doesn't want to hear. Instead of listening, it's not truly interested in the conversation or what the other person is saying. While the other person is talking, Little Brain waits for an opening so it can continue with what it wants to say.

Big Brain is interested in dialogue; Little Brain in monologues and not listening. Simon & Garfunkel put it well in their classic song "The Boxer," describing how some people choose not to hear what they don't want to hear.

What is said is not as important as what is heard. Listening with your Big Brain ensures that you'll hear the whole message and be better equipped to find the best answer. It also improves overall communication and relationships. When someone feels heard, they feel more connected to the person who is listening to them. True listening reinforces trust.

> **Listening** *is where control begins.*
> **Listening** *is where connection begins.*
> **Listening** *is where understanding begins.*

DON'T STEAL THE STORY'S MOMENT

In group discussions, someone will inevitably begin to tell a story. It is not uncommon but still rude for someone else to play one-upmanship—interrupting with what they believe is a better story. This is classic Little Brain behavior. It screams, "What about me?!" and reveals the interrupter to be immature or self-centered.

Some people are naturally great storytellers and may frequently get the limelight. Others may become jealous that someone else's stories always get the attention. However, any attempts to interrupt the storyteller or question or discredit parts of the story can be seen as jealousy.

Let the story be told.

In conversations involving several people, all too often, someone tries to steer the conversation to themselves. When you can recognize someone looking to steal the moment, you may need to help facilitate by guiding others to see that this conversation, this moment, is not about them. Here you can act as the designated conversation driver—keeping everyone focused on the real topic at hand and making sure the conversation does not spiral out of control, which would only leave a bruised Legacy.

THE FIRST EXPRESSION MAKES
THE FIRST IMPRESSION

How you arrive at an encounter communicates to others how you are feeling. At home, an encounter starts when you greet your loved ones. At work, it begins when you first notice a coworker or customer. In life, it happens the minute you walk around the corner or through a door. When you pick up your smartphone, encounters happen in the palm of your hand via texts, calls, or social media. Even if your routine is the same day after day, new encounters will present themselves regularly.

You know the wonderful feeling you experience when you're greeted warmly at a restaurant or a store? Likewise, you may have experienced the unhappy, insulted feeling you get when you're ignored. You return to those people and places that make you feel welcome, and you avoid the ones that don't. Online reviews, word-of-mouth advertising, and countless studies show: people go where they feel comfortable.

Not surprisingly, there's actual science behind this feeling of familiarity with people—even if you haven't met them before. Our limbic brain (the emotional one) actually "reads" the other person using visual and emotional cues. According to Dr. Henry Lodge in his book, *Younger Next Year*, "We read hundreds of subtle signals in each encounter: body language, tone of voice, flickers of facial expression" and other nuances of communication—then we create "emotional maps" in our brain that create an emotional attachment (or distance) to that person.

In other words, your tone, smile, attitude, body language, demeanor, manners, volume, and other signals tell the other person much more about you than just the words you're saying. And in some cases, your words aren't even heard above the booming signals you're giving off through other forms of expression.

You can turn even the smallest opportunity into a positive moment. A passing smile or quick eye contact can be a meaningful encounter. Be aware of how you walk into every encounter. Are you smiling? Are you wearing a frown leftover from a pressing problem moments ago—a frown that could easily be misinterpreted by a customer or coworker? It only takes a brief moment to check in with yourself, regain your awareness, and get to Neutral to prepare your Big Brain for the next moment.

AVOID OVERREACTING

We should always seek to avoid Little Brain reactions when communicating, and *overreacting* is even worse. Overreacting happens when you become so emotionally upset by a situation, a set of facts, or a provocation that you just can't think straight. Overreacting wears a hundred different masks. It may appear when you get upset over minor incidents or take the attitude of "I'll show them" in a conflict or disagreement. It can happen when you "kill the messenger"—blaming the bearer of bad news regardless of whether or not they have anything to do with it.

In the business world, overreacting can lead to loss—loss of income, loss of responsibilities, loss of prestige, and sometimes loss of a job. Overreacting at home creates divisions that can last for years if not addressed. Often relationships will have a difficult time recovering from frequent overreacting. These patterns are a sure indicator that Little Brain too often has too much control over you.

Ignoring a problem doesn't help, and overreacting to it creates its own set of problems. So the sweet spot in the middle becomes responding—thinking through appropriate actions to take or appropriate words to say to resolve a situation. When your Big Brain is in control, you can eliminate problems before they have a chance to fester.

"I JUST NEED TO GET BACK AT THEM."

Getting back at someone is perhaps one of the most prolific and destructive mistakes of communication.

It can show up in an instant, and before you know it, you've said something you wish you hadn't or done something you instantly regret. It feels right at the time—it may even feel justified, especially when someone has done or said something that offends you. You were activated and fell right into "Get Back."

With so many media outlets hosting forums for opposing opinion-makers to yell at each other or people snapping at each other on social media, the public is treated to a constant stream of Get Back with no time to truly listen, let alone seek a resolution. But two monologues do not make a dialogue. While the viewer or reader is looking for a discussion, these "debates" usually devolve into Get Back loops.

As you can see, this kind of communication leads nowhere but simply feeds on itself. It's an endless loop with each person thinking, *"Once I get back at the other person and have my say, then I will let it go."*

In one-on-one conversations in real life, that level of "debate" can escalate all too quickly. It can turn a disagreement into an argument and then into a confrontation, increasing the chances of a physical showdown. The idea that as soon as you say your piece, the negative interaction will end simply does not work. Getting back at someone does not end things. It escalates the situation.

HOW TO GET OUT OF THE GET BACK LOOP

This damaging, argumentative loop can continue almost forever, until one person remembers their Big Brain, realizes they are in the Get Back Loop, and says, "Let's look at this a different way," or "Maybe there is some common ground we can find."

Big Brain acknowledges the futility of continuing and finds a way to redirect the moment and escape the negative loop.

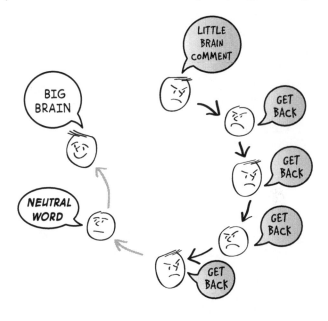

WIN-WIN THE MOMENT

In every communication moment, staying aware of the Legacy you might create, the Influences at hand, the possible pitfalls to avoid, and your overall goals for the conversation will keep you focused. Listening to the nuances of the encounter will keep you aware of how best to navigate that particular moment.

When provoked, you don't have to respond immediately. Regroup, look for the exit, invite your Little Brain to sit out this confrontation, and invite your Big Brain to take over. With your Big Brain in charge, you'll be able to see that winning the argument at hand may not leave the greatest Legacy. More important, your Big Brain knows how to still win the moment, making everyone involved feel this was a win-win moment.

TOOLS AND TRAPS OF CONTROL

While every communication moment is different, there are some common tools you can use to gain resolution and leave a favorable Legacy. There are also traps and pitfalls to avoid; recognize them, and Big Brain will have a better chance of winning the moment.

BIG BRAIN TOOL
NEUTRAL WORDS

TOOL

In the pressure of the moment, you may not immediately know exactly what to say or how to respond. These are the times your Neutral Word can be the most helpful. Use it to keep your Big Brain in control and prevent Little Brain from jumping in. When you're able to stay calm in tense situations, even in the presence of strong emotions, you can step back and become more aware of what this particular moment requires.

Instead of reacting to the Little Brain comments of others, assess and identify what Influences might be affecting them. Use friendly words and behavior to diffuse any tension.

LEGACY REWARDS

COMPOSED

OKAY, THAT IS ONE WAY TO LOOK AT IT.

TRAP

LITTLE BRAIN TRAP
CUTTING PEOPLE OFF

Finishing other people's sentences can be very tempting. Yet, cutting them off and assuming you know what (and how) they wanted to complete their thought lets others know you're impulsive. Little Brain is eager to express its opinion and not truly listen to anyone else. If someone needs assistance finding a word, they may appreciate the help, but this is a very tricky area. It's usually best to err on the side of patience. Let them finish their thought without your help.

RUDE

YEAH, YEAH, FINE, I KNOW WHAT YOU ARE TRYING TO SAY, BUT I...

BIG BRAIN TOOL
AUTHENTIC LISTENING

TOOL

The Austrian poet and pianist Alfred Brendel noticed something extraordinary that was actually in plain sight: the words "listen" and "silent" comprise the same letters. It's a great bit of trivia that will help you remember the only way to truly listen is to silence your thoughts—to quiet the impulsive need to react—so you can really hear what the other person is saying.

People notice how well you are paying attention to them. They know if you are using:

- Authentic listening: you're really paying attention
- Courtesy listening: out of politeness, not really there
- Superficial listening: just waiting for your time to speak

Try visualizing what the other person is saying as they speak. Look them in the eye. Your retention of the conversation will be greater, and your connection to that person will be much more powerful.

Avoid answering that text or looking away from the other person to check that alert. It can look like whatever is on the screen is more interesting than the person you're talking with. This digital multi-tasking is one of the greatest challenges to your ability to truly listen—to stay in the moment. It's eye contact that matters, not I-contact. Practice digital-free conversations whenever possible.

LEGACY REWARDS

ATTENTIVE

FASCINATING... I SEE WHAT YOU'RE TALKING ABOUT.

LITTLE BRAIN TRAP

TRAP

THE SPORT of FACT-CHECKING

With the power of infinite knowledge in our pockets today, it's not uncommon for some in a conversation to research a shared fact in real-time to find out if it is 100% accurate. This new phenomenon is also referred to as googling or know-it-all-itis.

For some people, fact-checking has become a sport. It's fine to keep people accountable and accurate, but interrupting the moment and their message can tell the speaker and those around you that you are not really interested in listening to what they have to say. Moreover, you leave a Legacy of doubt about the safety of having a conversation with you.

This is especially true when the "facts" you want to interject are not really relevant to the story or conversation. Let your Big Brain keep the urge to fact-check that little tidbit unspoken, and decide instead to look it up later. Only if it's an important detail would there be a reason to bring it up—and only then if it's the right time to do so.

KNOW-IT ALL-ITIS

LET ME GOOGLE THAT!

BIG BRAIN *BONUS* TOOL
SLIP THE PUNCH

TOOL

In the martial arts world, "slipping a punch" is the technique of letting the opponent throw their punch while you step out of the way. As your opponent throws their weight where they think you are, suddenly, you're not there. This allows you to maneuver and find a better spot to balance yourself for a response.

In communication, the same concept is useful: slipping a punch means letting an ignorant remark, a snide comment, a tacit insult, or even a direct verbal affront just slip by without letting it bother you. In most cases, it's almost always worth it to let it go. This is very handy with instigators.

For example, in a group gathering where many of the participants support different sports teams or political parties, a "my-team-is-better-than-your-team" comment usually surfaces. Perhaps, someone is looking to get under your skin. Slipping the punch in this case would mean simply letting the person make their comment without you responding. It's always advisable to ponder in Neutral for a little while, giving yourself time to ask the question, "Is this the right time, place, and audience for this discussion?"

CONTROL TAKEAWAY

No matter what happens in life, you have control of your responses and the consequences they can bring.

- Finding Neutral will help you navigate tough moments. Practice your Neutral Word or phrase until it becomes your default response.
- Beware of Get Back loops. Like quicksand, they are easy to get into and can be difficult to get out of, but you can always use Neutral to get out.
- Don't let your Little Brain do the talking.
- Truly listen to the other person.
- As technology becomes a greater part of our lives, and virtually every communication is recorded somewhere, it all adds up to our past. Keep in mind that your past will always be present on some device somewhere.
- The way to control your past is to keep Big Brain in control of the present.

"We often refuse to accept an idea
merely because the tone of voice
in which it has been expressed
is unsympathetic to us."

—Friedrich Nietzsche, philosopher,
cultural critic, and scholar

CHAPTER 8

PRINCIPLE 2:
TONE

"I LIKE THAT TONE BETTER, DADDY."

The power of a positive tone was one of the first lessons I learned in the journey that led me to creating *Big Brain Little Brain*. The lesson came from my daughter when she was very little. I'm proud to say that I learned a tremendous amount about communication from being the father of two wonderful girls. As in the workplace, the close interactions of the family environment provide us with limitless opportunities to grow or flounder.

When it comes to parenting, I have to admit to making many communication mistakes early on. I failed to pause and think when speaking with my children. I quickly learned, however, that I had an amazing amount of power to make moments go well, and the same amount of power to make them go wrong, simply by the way I handled each moment—and more specifically, by the tone I used.

One Christmas Eve, I was under the tree, stringing together lights, when I saw the little feet of my daughter, Katelyn, only seven at the time, start climbing the ladder I'd set up to hang decorations. Obviously, this wasn't safe, and I immediately adopted my parental tone of concern: "Katelyn," I said sternly, "get down from there."

She paused for a second and then continued on up. So I escalated my tone, getting slightly louder and adding her middle name. "Katelyn Rose. You get down."

She didn't respond. I was perplexed. Why wasn't she listening? This was unlike her.

THE BIG BRAIN RESPONSE

I got out from under the tree, on the verge of getting more upset seeing how high she was. In my Little Brain, I was ready to escalate my tone to Parental DEFCON 1.

I was ready to say, "Did you hear me? I said get down!"

But before I could utter those unpleasant words in an even more unpleasant tone, I noticed an angel in her hand that she was carrying to the top of the tree. I looked at her face and realized she was on the verge of tears.

I quickly switched to a much gentler tone. "Honey, I need you to get down. It's dangerous."

Sniffling, she said, "I like that tone better, Daddy."

I was floored.

"I just wanted to put the angel on top," she continued, with a catch in her voice.

Her desire to hang the angel was strong, and it meant a lot to her. She wanted to surprise me. Until I understood that this was what was influencing her behavior, I couldn't respond properly. I was using the wrong tone. I was definitely in Little Brain mode.

"I'll put it up there for you," I told her.

"But I want to do it myself," she said in a very small voice.

Humbled, I answered, "Okay, honey. But I will be right behind you because it's not safe for you to climb the ladder that high without someone holding you."

"Okay, Daddy."

Later that night, Katelyn came into the living room with her pajamas on. She looked at the top of the tree. She ran over to me and gave me one of the most powerful hugs in the history of hugs.

"Thank you, Daddy. She is a very pretty angel, isn't she?" I looked into my daughter's eyes. "Yes, she really is."

THE LITTLE BRAIN REACTION

If my parental need to overcontrol that moment had won the argument, I would have lost one of the most precious memories of my life. Instead, that moment—and many others like it with my daughters—led me to develop a better, more thoughtful communication style (many details of which have ended up put together here, in your hands).

ELEMENTS OF TONE

The story of the angel and the Christmas tree illustrates how the second principle, tone, plays out in everyday situations. When we react without assessing the other person's Influences or Activators, it's all too easy to react from our Little Brain. But the tone you use is always your choice.

THE TONE IS THE MESSAGE

As humans, we hear the tone of a communication even before our brain has time to process the meaning of the words. Just as we see and understand people's facial expressions before understanding their words, tone can be an audible smile or frown. It's the signal of a person's mood, and there are as many different tones as there are emotions. Identifying the particular tone being used by the other person is crucial to going beyond mere vocabulary and gaining clarity about what that person is really saying.

Infants begin learning to communicate with their parents by using tone. Long before we understand a single word, it's the tone of the people leaning over our cradles smiling, cooing, and laughing that helps us know how they feel. Babies can tell if their parents or caretakers are happy or sad, frightened or tired. Likewise, our first language is tone. Before we form the words to communicate what we need, we converse purely in tones. Our caretakers learn the nuances of these tones to decipher whether we need to eat, are missing a sock, or are curious about something we've just noticed.

As we grow up, we begin connecting words with tones, but even as our vocabularies expand, we never lose the ability to read a tone by itself. You can even tell when the same word spoken in different tones means something entirely different. Throughout our lives, the tone with which you deliver a message continues to be more important than the words themselves in getting that message across.

> *We hear the tone of a communication*
> *even before our brain has time to process*
> *the meaning of the words.*

TONE BRINGS FEELINGS

Tone is one of the strongest indications you'll get about whether a person—including yourself—is coming from their Big Brain or Little Brain. Little Brain reactions and tones tend to escalate in both volume and intensity. Big Brain tones are usually softer and calmer, and have an underlying strength. They lay the foundation for a smooth exchange. A sustained Big Brain tone can be a powerful inducement to others in the conversation to follow. World-class marathon runner Paula Radcliffe once said, "You can be strong and true to yourself without being loud or rude."

However, when you are frustrated, annoyed, uncomfortable, or uneasy, the possibility of using Little Brain tones increases. If no one else in the exchange is coming from their Big Brain, those Little Brain tones will get louder and louder, and the temptation to match the current tone, or even up the ante, will rise. Negative tones can continue to escalate until an argument ensues, leaving a poor Legacy or turning an encounter into a confrontation.

Little Brain tones, like air in a balloon, expand and expand. They might start as annoyance or frustration and grow in negativity as the moment continues. Ultimately, the Little Brain tone balloon bursts—and that's never a happy result.

Though Big Brain tones are less loud and showy, they can actually be more powerful. They have an undercurrent of strength, calm, and ease. They can draw people to them, even in the presence of Little Brain intonation. While Little Brain tones are a swelling balloon, Big Brain tones are a steady, solid foundation for positive communication. Holding on to Big Brain tones even while others are using Little Brain tones is a sign of maturity and strength.

It's easy to pick up bad tones—like picking up bad habits. You hear Little Brain tones from other people or in movies and other media. The tones get packed away but stay around, waiting to be used by your Little Brain at will. Fortunately, good tones can also become a part of your habits. The challenge is to make sure your Big Brain tone wins the race in the comment about to be made. Compassionate, sincere, and calm tones will serve you well in any communication.

Everyone, no matter how old or young, understands tone. In business or at home, the tone you use will convey the message more than your words. In any communication, the tone is the message.

YOUR ANCHOR TONE

Before approaching any known encounter, especially if it's a tough one, it's a good idea to establish the anchor tone you want to use. An anchor tone is your central tone for the conversation. Sincerity is a good, basic anchor tone, but there are others, too. For example, in a serious conversation, you may want to add a tone of concern. In a lighthearted situation, a whimsical tone might be more appropriate. Maybe you need to add a more optimistic tone. If the tone has escalated to aggravated or annoyed, you can come back to a steady, sincere, calm tone—one of peacemaking. Whichever tone you choose, it will be remembered long after the words are forgotten.

The tone you use to open the conversation indicates the attitude you are bringing to the moment—so choose your anchor tone wisely. Align your tone with your smile. Let your smile lead the way and anchor the moment.

WHAT IS YOUR DIGITAL TONE?

Establishing and maintaining an appropriate tone is even trickier in written or digital communication, especially in emails and texts. Electronic messages may be terrific for sharing specific pieces of information, but when it comes to conveying tone, they're often disasters waiting to happen. It has become very common to communicate in the short, choppy, unemotional, and flat tones of the digital world. These toneless communications are no replacement for your voice and presence.

Take a moment to look back over your recent texts and emails to see how you "speak" in the digital world. If the typos don't scare you, the tone quality should. And using emojis? While those little indicators of expression are becoming more expansive and elaborate, they still don't completely deliver the tone as well as you would with your own voice or in person. When a message is sensitive, it might be better to deliver it not in writing but in "voice."

TOOLS AND TRAPS OF TONE

The sound of your voice can communicate so much more than the ideas you want to express in the moment. In fact, the brain processes sound differently than visual cues or even words spoken—giving tone an even greater power.

Of course, while every moment is different, there are some common tools you can use to master your tone and traps to watch out for.

BIG BRAIN TOOL
PLEASANT TONE

Maintaining a pleasant tone is a powerful Tool. In its own way, this Tool has the amazing ability to diffuse tense situations and keep everyone focused. When you remain calm and use the tone that matches your desired results, you create an atmosphere that supports clarity for all. When you hear the tone around you changing or escalating, your unwavering, steady tone will reset the conversation and bring others to your level.

From this balanced position, you'll be better able to:

- Read the tones of other people to gauge what their Influences might be.
- Understand what they are really communicating beneath their words.
- Create an environment that has a soothing impact on any moment.

TOOL

LEGACY REWARDS
ENJOYABLE

HELLO THERE!

LITTLE BRAIN TRAP

ESCALATION

Escalation occurs when people confuse loudness with power. They think that the louder they are, the more power they have—and they continually try to one-up the tone or volume of others. Unfortunately, when you both reach the limits of loudness, the struggle to be the most powerful can turn confrontational.

But loudness is only the illusion of power. What it actually reveals is weakness, trying to mask insecurity with volume.

This is a good time to stay away from clichés. They each have a tone and are easily misunderstood.

Clichés are a good alert for yourself, too, to recognize that it's not you speaking anymore; it's just an expression you've heard someone else use. Clichés come with a baggage tone all their own, no matter how you might have meant it, and are likely to escalate the tone of the discourse.

TRAP

THOUGHTLESS

SOMEONE WOKE UP ON THE WRONG SIDE OF THE BED!

BIG BRAIN TOOL
SMILING EYES

TOOL

The eyes are the window to the soul, which makes them very powerful. They connect you immediately with others, so you can create a genuine expression of comfort and welcome by making sure your eyes are in alignment with your tone. They reveal your sincerity. Be sure your eyes reflect a true smile. Smiling eyes make people comfortable and express your intent to engage in a friendly exchange.

LEGACY REWARDS

FRIENDLY

LITTLE BRAIN TRAP

FROWNING

Physical cues are also a part of tone. Rolling your eyes, wearing an annoyed or unconcerned expression, smirking, a furrowed brow—these all indicate that the listener doesn't truly want to participate in the conversation. Sometimes, you may not even think you're frowning but have carried over feelings from a previous moment in your expression. Wherever they're coming from, frowns can be easily misinterpreted. They can show that you're not truly interested in the energy of the moment and want to be somewhere else.

DISRESPECTFUL

GET S.E.T.—PUTTING IT ALL TOGETHER

TOOL

You might have all the layers of clothes you need, matched your shoes to your bag, and even remembered to press your shirt, but as the old saying goes, you're never fully dressed without a smile. A smile is free to wear, and the return on the effort is invaluable.

When you Get S.E.T. for each moment, you'll reap these benefits:

- A **SMILE** sends a positive message with your facial expression.
- **EYE CONTACT** shows you are personally engaged in the conversation.
- Choosing a good **TONE** lays the vocal foundation for the encounter.

From the first few seconds of the exchange, people will be able to see you aren't superficially going through the motions but are sincere and in the moment with them.

LEGACY REWARDS

WELCOMING

S.
E.
T.

TONE TAKEAWAY

Tone is a powerful element of any communication. It signals to others what mood you are in or what intentions you have. It overpowers any words uttered.

The same words spoken in a different tone have a different meaning. The tone is the message. Whether the communication is spoken in words, facial expressions, texts, posts, or any other messages, it has a tone. You always have the ability to set the tone of a moment and reset the tone throughout any encounter.

Before an encounter, choose the tone you will use to anchor your message, such as calm, pleasant, or caring. How do you want this message to be remembered?

"Words are, of course, the most powerful drug used by mankind."

—Rudyard Kipling, author of *The Jungle Book* and winner of the Nobel Prize for Literature

CHAPTER 9

PRINCIPLE 3:
WORDS

GOOD GOSSIP

Robert is a manager at a busy retail store in Manhattan. The store is part of a larger chain, yet does its best to keep the neighborhood charm. Robert became the manager when the store was having trouble with expenses exceeding income. His work ethic, his long days, and his new systems helped turn the store around.

Angela was a longtime saleswoman at the same store. She had been there much longer than Robert, but she never wanted to be anything other than a salesperson, tending to her regular customers as though they were her friends. The place felt like home. She was not fond of the new systems and rules when they were implemented, but she understood their need and followed them completely. She was more comfortable on the floor of the shop than anywhere else.

Over the years, Robert and Angela began to be short with each other. There was no single incident; no one particular thing that created the rift. They just both had strong personalities, and their conversations became corporate-like and abrupt.

As the tension grew, they stopped speaking to each other except when absolutely necessary. The rest of the staff noticed this awkwardness. It was beginning to have an impact on the atmosphere in the store. Their morning greeting to each other turned to annoyed expressions of acknowledgment. No words were spoken.

Patricia, the district manager, began to hear about this situation from other employees and took notice. She tried talking to each of them, but each said it was really not a problem. Still, the same pattern continued.

One day, as the end of the quarter approached, it was time for an all-staff meeting. Angela had personal plans she couldn't change that day and was excused from the meeting. Patricia decided she would take advantage of the opportunity and try something. The day before the meeting, she called Robert into her office. "Robert, I need you to do me a favor."

Robert said, "Sure. What is it?"

"First, can you think of three things Angela does well?"

Robert rolled his eyes. "Well, I can certainly find three things she could do better."

Patricia looked at him, smiled, and waited.

Robert got the message. "Yes, I can find three things she does well. She is always on time, she dresses well, and she is great with customers, especially the difficult ones."

"Perfect!" said Patricia. "Now, here's the favor. Tomorrow at the staff meeting, after you go through your regular items, I want you to take a moment to highlight those three things that Angela does well. Compliment her in front of the crew while she is not there. Then end the meeting on that positive note."

Robert frowned. "Are you sure that's a good idea?"

"Yes, I really am."

"Okay, but I'm not sure what good it will do."

THE BIG BRAIN RESPONSE

At the meeting, Robert ran over the details about store performance and discussed the goals for the next quarter. Then he ended with, "By the way, I just want to take this opportunity to say something about Angela. Angela has been here for so long that I don't know if we really appreciate how good she is at what she does. We can all take note of how great she is on the floor. She is always on time and impeccably dressed, and the way she handles the tough customers is really something to watch. I have to say the store is stronger because she is here." He then ended the meeting with, "Thank you all for coming. Let's get ready to open."

Patricia was amazed. After the meeting, she told Robert, "Not even I was ready for that strong of a speech! That was very sincere. You really came through."

"It felt kind of good," he replied sheepishly. "But why did you have me do that?"

Patricia smiled. "We'll see."

The next day, Robert arrived at the store a little early. Angela was already behind the counter, watching as Robert walked to unlock the front door to let a customer in. Then, from behind the counter, came something Robert had not heard in a long time, and never in such an upbeat tone.

"Good morning, Robert."

He turned to see Angela with a smile on her face.

"Good morning, Angela!" he replied enthusiastically. "Very nice to see you!"

"You too, Robert."

Later that day in the hallway, Robert and Angela passed each other with a smile. Angela stopped and gave Robert a big hug. Then without a word, she returned to her station. As it turns out, his "Good Gossip" about Angela had spread throughout the store in less than twenty-four hours.

Robert learned an important lesson in management that day: what you say about people gets repeated. Introducing Good Gossip not only impacted Robert and Angela's relationship, but it improved the atmosphere in the store, as well as the attitude of the rest of the team. They began to wonder what nice things were said about them when they weren't there. They all started saying nice things about each other; it rebooted a culture of team and family. By wholeheartedly taking Patricia's advice, that one moment became a complete turnaround for the whole store, and it became one of the company's best performing locations.

THE LITTLE BRAIN REACTION

Let's take a look at the outcome that a Little Brain reaction might have created.

At the meeting, if Robert had said nothing about Angela, their relationship would have continued to deteriorate. Or worse, he might have blurted out something snarky and disrespectful at the meeting instead and created a negative atmosphere for the entire team.

The tension between Robert and Angela would have escalated, poisoning the environment in the store and eventually becoming obvious to shoppers and vendors. The store would have lost business, but more importantly, Robert and Angela would have lost the sense of accomplishment and growth.

ELEMENTS OF WORDS

Poor communication in work environments is far too common. But it doesn't take a district manager to suggest ways to turn it around. Anyone can start sharing Good Gossip—using the power of words to create change. Think about your own office dialog for a moment. Do you use positive, affirming words—or do you add to the negative attitude with words that are unhelpful or even unkind? The words you use are always your choice.

Home communication environments have the same characteristics. In fact, it's helpful to understand how the use of Good Gossip and positive comments can improve relationships in both places since what happens at work has an impact on one's home environment, and one's home environment has an impact at work.

THE POWER OF WORDS

Words are free. Collect as many good ones as you can. A weak vocabulary leaves us bankrupt in a conversation that needs more words than we have to spend. Gather and save good words as you would anything of value, to be carefully utilized later.

Words are also critical when it comes to crafting the right message. The power of communication is entirely in your hands. You get to choose the words that you're going to use. You get to choose exactly when you use them. And you get to choose how you use them.

While there are more than 170,000 words in the English language to choose from, most people have a vocabulary of 20,000–30,000 words, yet many use less than 10,000 of these in their daily lives.

No matter how many words you use, your Big Brain and Little Brain have the same access to all of them. Both brains are in a constant struggle to grab words and get them out faster than the other. But Big Brain wants to think first and choose its words carefully, while Little Brain is comfortable spitting out something fast. Little Brain, as we've learned, is closer to your mouth. This proximity gives it a greater chance to get a reactionary comment out first. So Big Brain must be ready with some quick messages of its own or at least be ready to go quickly into Neutral before Little Brain has a chance to react.

> You get to **choose** the words that you're going to use.
> You get to **choose** exactly when you use them.
> And you get to **choose** how you use them.

SPRING-LOADED WORDS

Imagine our Big Brain and Little Brain each having a spring-loaded compartment for quick access to words and phrases—ready to jump out and be the first to say something.

Big Brain's storage compartment is filled with positive words and comments to reinforce the moment. It's very comfortable with something that the Little Brain isn't—a moment of silence. Big Brain knows that sometimes silence and reflection can be an entirely appropriate response, especially when you need time to think things through and consider your words.

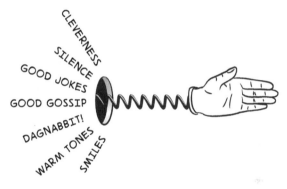

The spring-loaded Big Brain is ready with positive comments at a moment's notice.

Little Brain's storage compartment, on the other hand, is stuffed with pent-up phrases, building under pressure and desperately looking for their next chance to get out. It's filled with every negative comeback, insult, snide remark, cliché, and inappropriate reaction you've ever contemplated. Little Brain is terrified of silence. Its reflexes tell it to fill the silence, whether or not it's the right time—or the right words to do so.

NAME-CALLING
GOSSIP
OOPS
INSULTS
SLURS
SARCASM

The spring-loaded Little Brain is ready with negative comebacks and remarks.

BETTER VOCABULARY, BETTER CHOICES

We already know the lasting impact a comment can have, good or bad, and the Legacy it leaves. We also know that everything you say will usually be heard by everyone. Communication today makes its way around the world at light speed. That velocity can be dangerous.

In an episode of *Downton Abbey*, the Countess of Grantham, played by the magnificent Maggie Smith, exemplifies one who chooses her words carefully. At a family function, a crude comment is made by someone hoping to be funny, but it is not received as humorous. She turns to the person and eloquently says, "Vulgarity is no substitute for wit."

Society has become much more casual in the century since Countess Grantham's time. But even a generation ago, people in "polite society" never used the slang and profanities that have become regular staples of speech today. However, the value of politeness is still paramount. It's not just the words themselves that make a difference, but also how we use them. Manners, at their core, are simply being considerate of others' feelings. The words may change, but we can always cultivate that polite attitude. It's surprising to see individuals, even in positions of power and Influence, give little thought to the words they choose and the damage they can cause. Your wording represents you, and those word choices create a Legacy.

MAKE A LIST

If you hit your thumb with a hammer by accident, letting out a string of four-letter words is probably the least of your concerns. If you're by yourself, it might be no problem; in fact, it may actually be healthy to let it out, and loudly. But if you're not alone, using loud tones or foul language can leave a poor Legacy. Often these words have become a habit and can seem hard to break. But remember, it wasn't always a habit; you may have picked up those words from others along the way, and you can choose to leave them behind. Given time, you can actually retrain your now-automatic responses to instead use words that are more likely to be appropriate in any scenario.

Make a list of the top ten bad words you know. Keep it close by for now. How often do you find yourself using them?

Using foul language for added effect or to put others down is a definitive mark of Little Brain (and immaturity). The specific words that are considered profane may vary depending on the environment, but there are always some hot-button choices that are almost sure to offend.

You can still let off steam—just choose different words when others are present. Some Big Brain communicators even warn others they are just venting for a minute.

DON'T PASS IT ON

Bad words can quickly identify negative intent. Often they are used to be more dramatic as if their shock value adds power to one's word choice. It does not. Little Brain uses profanity when you could use better, more creative words to spice up your message. Before long, using such words becomes part of the way you speak. Those words highlight ignorance, not power.

Passing on the foul language that someone else uses is almost as bad as using it yourself. The more these poorly chosen words are uttered, the more accepted they become in general, and the more they get used by others.

Now take the list of bad words you created above. Four-lettered or not, for each bad word you wrote down, find a suitable replacement word that won't be offensive. You could even expand your list and replace all the bad words you know—for example, replacing "stupid" with "foolish." Or replacing "clueless" with "unfamiliar," and so on.

You can even turn it into a game, finding unusual or rarely used words to make your case. Have you tried "indiscreet," "cranky," "disproportionate," or "ineffectual," for example?

REDISCOVERING SALUTATIONS

Decades ago, every letter started with Dear Mrs. Smith or Dear Dr. Marshall. But today, the world of texting, tweets, and posts has stripped away many of these opening salutations—and the practice is beginning to work its way into emails, memos, and even letters in the business world. Instead, people are rushing straight to the information with little communication or greeting.

Unfortunately, when you begin an encounter without an opening salutation, you risk leaving the gap open to the other person's interpretation. Especially in written communication, readers are left to assume a tone, and often they may assume the wrong one.

Likewise, when you close a message without saying some variation of good-bye, ending it abruptly, the reader will be left feeling unclear or possibly insulted. This is a hallmark of Little Brain behavior—often leaving a conversation without the proper salutation and leaving a Legacy of being crude or careless on departure.

Big Brain knows that, when starting and ending an encounter, what you say first and what you say last leaves an impression. In written correspondence, your opening salutation is the smile in text that says hello in place of a welcoming facial expression and friendly tone. Writing some version of "hello" and "good-bye" in all forms of digital communications will open and close moments with a positive tone. When you leave a voice mail, be sure to use a positive tone that is clearly understood. Sometimes just a nice tone at the end of a voice mail will be enough to make the listener smile. Big Brain leads and leaves with a friendly hello and good-bye.

TOOLS AND TRAPS OF WORDS

The words you use can empower someone, improve their outlook, and calm a situation—or they can do just the opposite. It's always your choice. Luckily, there are some common tools you can use to improve your word usage and communication style— leading to a better reputation. There are also traps to watch for.

BIG BRAIN TOOL
GOOD GOSSIP

TOOL

In every encounter, the first thing to do is assess who is in the room. Knowing who is there and likely to hear the conversation will help you navigate the conversation. However, whatever you say in the room may very likely be repeated later to others who aren't in the room. Any comment—good or bad—said about someone will eventually be heard by everyone. Maybe not right away, but they will hear about it. Good Gossip and bad gossip travel the same path, but they have very different results.

So who is really in the room? Everyone.

Used wisely—and with a little effort—Good Gossip can inspire those who hear it. As listeners hear your comments about the positive traits of others, they will focus on their own positive traits with the knowledge others could be paying attention to them, too. Good Gossip plants seeds of success.

LEGACY REWARDS
GRACIOUS

GINA GETS ALONG WITH EVERYBODY AND SHE GETS A LOT DONE.

TRAP

LITTLE BRAIN TRAP
Gossip Bullies

Bullies pick on the weak, and there is no one weaker than someone who is not in the room to defend themselves. Gossip Bullies often use under-the-breath comments, texts, private chat areas, private channels, or other dark corners of interaction. These hidden gutters of communication are a stealthy way of undermining someone without their knowledge. Behind-the-back avenues are often used by those who lack the courage to speak face-to-face because their comments would not survive scrutiny.

The biggest outcome of this behind-the-scenes behavior—for the bully—is that they become untrustworthy in other people's eyes. If this behavior describes someone you know, realize what others are thinking: *If he says those things about Timothy behind his back, what's he saying about me when I'm not around?*

There is no way to completely eliminate Gossip Bullies from your life, but you can take care not to pass on or forward the information Gossip Bullies put out. Don't participate in the gossip chain. You are a conduit of communication, and what you say or pass on about others reveals far more about your discretion than it does about them.

UNDERMINING

YOU KNOW WHAT I HEARD ABOUT HER...

BIG BRAIN TOOL
C-TO-C RATIO

TOOL

Compliments and critiques are regular pieces of communication and particularly common in constructive communication, professional or personal. As you embark on the encounters of your day, be sure to keep your compliment-to-critique ratio (C-to-C ratio) properly balanced.

Sometimes, people offer "words of wisdom" about situations others are experiencing: "What you need to do is..." Offering advice when someone is not asking for help can sometimes come across as criticism. Most people take critiques pretty well—if they come in doses they can handle and from people they trust. If there are no genuine compliments or honestly positive comments to balance out those critiques, it can sound like the other person only finds fault in what they do.

This is especially true with people you know the best. Partners and family can be notoriously critical, for example. While you might believe you're helping them by pointing out a mistake or detailing how they can do something better— while you might want to give them advice about a decision they're contemplating—too many critiques can feel negative. And often, with those people we know the best, we forget to balance those bits of "advice" with encouragement.

The balance of your C-to-C ratio should always be heavily weighted on the side of sincere, worthwhile compliments. Eighty/twenty is a good rule here.

If you truly desire to have a good communication relationship with someone, keep the compliments top of mind for easy use and the critiques to an effective minimum. Once you have used up your quota of critiques on any one person for the moment, it would be beneficial to hand out some compliments before any more critiques are issued.

LEGACY REWARDS
THOUGHTFUL

ROOM FOR A FEW IMPROVEMENTS

I LOVE YOUR WORK!

THAT'S SO NICE OF YOU!

GREAT JOB!

CRITIQUE

COMPLIMENT

TRAP

LITTLE BRAIN TRAP

NAME-CALLING

Little Brain likes to make fun of others. Bad jokes and name-calling, however, spread like gossip. A bad joke's journey will eventually lead it to the person who will be most offended by it.

The temptation to be funny is powerful. Yet in an increasingly sensitive world, it's wise to recognize that what may seem funny to you and those around you is not always funny to others. Too often, you may think a joke is funny or clever in the moment, but you later realize it was inappropriate. Be sure to keep the humor away from areas of sensitivity and any labels that could appear as name-calling.

ABRASIVE

HE IS
SUCH a
@#$%*¢ !

BIG BRAIN *BONUS* TOOL

AND THEN THERE IS "YOU"

TOOL

No word is more personal than "you." When "you" comes out of your mouth, it's best if it is followed by a compliment. Before using the worn-out and almost always inaccurate phrases "you always," "you never," "you'd better," and "you have to" or other comments where "you" is used to attack someone, stop to see if Little Brain is in control of the conversation. If so, take a moment, and choose a positive Big Brain word or two.

"You" should always be followed by a positive comment or even a sincere compliment. It's a very personal word. Use it correctly.

LEGACY REWARDS

CONSIDERATE

YOU ROCK!

WORDS TAKEAWAY

The words we use define us. A stronger vocabulary gives us more choices in how we respond.

- Words have a ripple effect long after they are spoken.
- Your ability to choose the right words and refrain from using the wrong ones will have a lasting impact on both personal and career relationships.
- Good Gossip will benefit the culture at home and at work. Look for good things to say about someone when they are not present. It speaks to who you are as a person and builds trust with everyone who hears you.
- Compliments should always outnumber complaints and critiques. The balance is critical to keeping people open to listening to you and keep them feeling like they can trust you.
- "Hello" and "good-bye" add a personal touch.

"If we take care of the moments, the
years will take care of themselves."

—Maria Edgeworth, social commentary
writer in nineteenth-century
England and Ireland

CHAPTER 10

PRINCIPLE 4:
TIME

MARY'S VERY LONG DAY

Mary had a rough day at work. She works as a dental hygienist, and that day, she was overscheduled. In the middle of the day, with the waiting room filled with people, the office's computer system failed. Mary and the receptionist worked hard to keep the appointments flowing smoothly, but inevitably, things got backed up. Mary felt the full force of her patients' irritation after they'd been kept waiting an hour or longer. She did not take lunch in an attempt to keep things from backing up even more.

When she finally left work and headed to pick up her son Sam from kindergarten, she was tired, worn out, and hungry. Sam, on the other hand, had loved his day. His teacher had shown the class how to use construction paper and magazine clippings to make a collage, and he was eager to show his mother his project.

Immediately after Mary buckled Sam into the back seat and got behind the wheel, he started calling, "Mommy! Mommy! Look in my backpack!"

Mary was elsewhere. She was thinking about how much she wanted to get home, have something to eat, and relax. She had already started the car and was pulling away from the curb and into traffic. She couldn't drive and rummage around in Sam's backpack at the same time. She felt herself tense up.

THE BIG BRAIN RESPONSE

Mary paused a moment and went into Neutral before replying to Sam in the back seat. Sam had no idea what Mary had dealt with that day. He was simply excited about his project and wanted to share that excitement with his mom. She smiled at her son in the rearview mirror.

Mary chose to explain in a very sincere tone, "Sam, I bet you have something really special to show me, and I can't wait to see it. But I can't look at it while I'm driving, so I have to ask you to be patient a little longer. How about we wait until we get home? That's the first thing we will do!"

Sam smiled in agreement.

All she had to do was pause, go to Neutral, and evaluate a split-second longer, and her Big Brain kicked in with the thoughtful, appropriate, and positive response that Sam needed and appreciated.

Fortunately, Mary's Big Brain took control. Her Big Brain wanted to share his important project with him, and she used the right tone of voice under the pressure of the moment to give Sam the message he needed.

Despite the day's outside Influences, Mary's core was strong enough and allowed her to win a precious moment with Sam.

THE LITTLE BRAIN REACTION

The outcome of this moment could have been very different if she had let Little Brain take control.

An exhausted and hungry Mary overreacted and said, "Just sit down and let me drive." Sam, scared by her sharp tone, became sad and withdrawn. He sat silently the whole drive home. When they got home, he had lost his desire to show Mary his work. And Mary lost the opportunity for a wonderful moment to share in her son's pride in his schoolwork.

ELEMENTS OF TIME

The world is moving at a faster pace than even five years ago. With so many demands on us, it's difficult to make the time to be courteous, generous, gracious, and thoughtful. But these are the hallmarks of Big Brain communication.

TIME IS ON YOUR SIDE

Of all the Influences in life, time often feels like the most difficult to manage. But it's really the one you have the *most* control over.

Time is perfectly consistent. Twenty-four hours is always twenty-four hours. That doesn't change. What changes are the circumstances that you create for yourself during those hours. When you overschedule your life, you create situations that make it seem as if time is working against you. If you pack too many activities into too little time, you'll get stressed and become far more likely to use your Little Brain.

But if you let time know how you want to spread out your activities, it will be there to help you organize. In reality, time is your friend. It's a tool when you use it to your advantage and a major trap when you let it get the best of you.

Plan for enough time to accomplish what you want to accomplish. If you don't, you make time your master.

> *In reality, time is your friend.*
> *It's a tool when you use it to your advantage and a*
> *major trap when you let it get the best of you.*

TIMING IT

In any communication, you can use the right words, use the correct tone, and even be calm and in control, but if you choose a bad time to start the conversation, the encounter might still end up with a negative Legacy. It may leave you wishing you had simply waited for a better time to deliver your comments.

We can all fall into the trap of bad timing when we force an issue or question on others because it fits our schedule—without pausing to ask ourselves if it's the right time to address it— or when we make even well-meaning suggestions at an insensitive time. For instance, we've all made untimely comments, like bringing up someone's unhealthy diet just as he or she is taking a bite of a hamburger—or adding to others' anxieties by burdening them with new problems at a difficult time. Little Brain disregards good timing and leaves a Legacy of being thought-less or even mean.

There's a time and a place for everything.

It's good timing for parents to speak to their children about how they should only accept good treatment from others—and how they should treat others respectfully—long before their first date. Don't wait until minutes before your teenager is walking out the door to impart your words of wisdom.

It's poor timing to tell someone about a crucial meeting on the day of the event. Similarly, you don't want to deliver bad news to people in front of others. An intuitive individual is courteous enough to take someone aside and privately deliver whatever comment or criticism needs to be expressed.

Good timing is also known as "tact." You're tactful when you embrace the art of waiting. Choosing the optimum time to have an encounter keeps the outcome and Legacy in mind. Ask yourself, *When is the best time to have this discussion?* Also, it's important to understand that others may not be ready to accept what you have to say right at that moment. Big Brain is conscientious and mindful of choosing the best timing for the communication.

CONNECTED OR TETHERED?
THE PERILS OF SOCIAL MEDIA

In an era of exploding social media, many of our encounters never really end. They're moving at an increased pace that gives us less and less time to formulate a response. Often, this snappy communication results in reactions and messages we might want to take back.

British actress Emma Watson acknowledged the perils of trying to do too many things at once when she tweeted, "I just dropped my iPhone in my soup. I think it might be time to tone down the multitasking."

In addition to speed, the sheer number of conversations we have going on at once has increased dramatically. Managing these multiple conversations—and the multiple moments and their legacies—requires us to develop an entirely new set of skills to keep our Big Brain in control.

Certainly, electronic tools have their good points. Technology can quickly deliver needed information, and it can also be a handy way for parents to stay connected to their children (and grandchildren), for friends and family to stay in touch, and for organizations to communicate important messages to their members.

Like any tool, though, if misused, it can do incredible damage.

Multitasking can compromise our conversations if we're not careful. Although we might be exchanging information with a number of people, can we say that we are truly communicating? Are we engaged and paying attention? Are we sure we're creating the feelings we want to create? And are we responding or simply reacting?

One of the realities of modern technology is the assumption that because other people can communicate with us instantly, we must somehow respond with equal speed. Try as we might to manage our schedule, the expectation of an instant response is rampant. Unfortunately, too many of us feel pressured to comply, even though there may be Influences and Activators affecting our ability to use our Big Brain in that moment. This is exactly the time when Little Brain gets us into trouble by causing us to craft hasty, short responses that we don't even read before sending. Even worse, a text or email may not even be the best method to respond. Perhaps a phone call or a face-to-face meeting would be better.

Take a moment to ponder if the tool you're using is the right one for the message you're about to send. Do you need more time to craft a response? Should you communicate using a different method? Digital moments create perfect opportunities for the Little Brain to creep in.

THE "OOPS" PRINCIPLE

When you are writing a letter by hand or on your keyboard, you can always look at it before you mail it and say, "Oops, that's not how I should say that." In the digital realm, unfortunately, once the message has been sent, there is little to no chance to erase it successfully—and even with email programs that let you "unsend" or which have a delay feature, there's no guarantee it's 100 percent recoverable.

If only there were an "oops" button.

Given the velocity of messages coming at us in so many forms, it's all too natural and understandable to go into a high-speed messaging mode. Unfortunately, when we do, we aren't taking the time to consider that each of these messages constitutes a moment and will create a Legacy. And for better or worse, a permanent one.

Reacting quickly can be a setup for disaster. When someone sends you a text, email, or voice mail, you might think you have to respond immediately. You don't. Never feel as though you've got to toss back every one of those messages with a prompt response, like a professional juggler who can't let anything hit the floor. Especially when our Little Brains are activated, we may feel the urge to send an angry text, or send an emotional email (and cc everyone), or broadcast our negative thoughts and feelings on social media. Instead of hitting the "send" button, get to Neutral. Take time to think about your response and be sure of it before you send it off. Once you push "send," that's it—your time to edit is over.

THE QUICK APOLOGY

What can you do if an "oops" moment occurs? A quick apology prevents long-term damage.

We all slip up once in a while and say the wrong thing or do something that, in hindsight, we wish we had handled differently. Although we know better, in the pressure of the moment, Little Brain creeps in and creates a negative ripple effect.

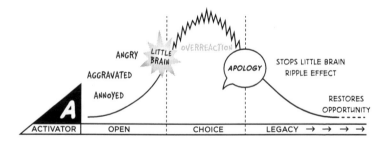

LITTLE BRAIN MOMENTS HAPPEN,
APOLOGY SMOOTHS LEGACY

The good news is that a quick apology can smooth out the long-term impact of most Little Brain Moments. Here are a few examples:

- "You know, I probably should have handled that better. Apologies, I did not mean to say that."

- "Please forgive my careless reaction."
- "I am sorry I did not think about your feelings when I said that."

These phrases or others that you create can help prevent long-term negative impact. Any Little Brain "oops" moment often can be smoothed out with a quick apology that restores the opportunity to continue the relationship.

TOOLS AND TRAPS OF TIME

Exercising caution in the timing of when you deliver bad news or new demands helps you stay in Big Brain mode and in control of every situation. Moreover, not letting your own schedule impact your communications makes you a thoughtful, mature, levelheaded, and reliable person at home and in the workplace. Whether you react quickly with your Little Brain or respond after properly considering the situation (a Big Brain habit), it's always your choice. The tools for Big Brain thinkers and traps for Little Brain hotheads are numerous.

TAKE CHARGE OF YOUR CALENDAR

TOOL

Organize your time to help you communicate. You know your own needs and to-do items; schedule your day, week, month, and year. Creating ample time for responding to communications from others will allow you to communicate on your terms, never rushed or last minute. Do not allow others to decide how to spend your time. Sudden phone calls, emails, and invites can seem overly important, and before you know it, your agenda for the day has been handed to others. Protect your schedule like you would a bank account. This asset is irreplaceable.

LEGACY REWARDS

ORGANIZED

LET ME SEE IF I CAN FIT THAT IN...

TRAP

LITTLE BRAIN TRAP
LoSiNG PATiENCE

Waiting in traffic, shopping, waiting for others to meet you before you can move on, hurrying to get to work, waiting in a long line at the coffee house, needing information and not getting it fast enough—moments like these are Little Brain territory.

When you feel yourself full of anxiety for something you cannot immediately control and begin to lose patience, tap into Neutral and ask a few questions: *Why am I rushing? Is there really an urgency here? Is it worth overreacting?* Questions are a great path into Neutral.

More often than not, we can afford to wait a little longer.

IMPETUOUS

COME ON! WHAT'S THE HoLDUP?

BIG BRAIN TOOL
TELEGRAPHING

TOOL

We don't send telegraphs to communicate anymore, but it's a great metaphor for giving advance notice. Sometimes, you must inform those close to you of impending change by conveying important information well in advance. There's a huge difference between saying, "From now on, we will do things differently," which doesn't give people enough time to understand and accept the change, and saying something like, "Starting next month, we're going to approach things differently."

Telegraphing empowers people to adapt. Telegraphing involves the art of seeing an upcoming event, circumstance, or occurrence and giving others enough time to process and accept the change. It may be a discussion on cutting expenses, a job change, new policies, a major deadline, a large family event, or new rules of the house. Telegraph anything that will take people out of what is familiar, routine, and comfortable to them. This will allow processing time for them to accept the circumstances and make the most of what's happening.

LEGACY REWARDS

DIPLOMATIC

NEXT MONTH, WE'RE CHANGING THE SCHEDULE.

LITTLE BRAIN TRAP

TRAP

AMBUSHING

When you fall into the Ambush Trap, you punish yourself and those around you by pushing demands on people who are not expecting them or are unprepared to handle them in the moment. Ambushes are never appreciated.

You ambush people when you:

- Lack discretion and bring up a sensitive topic in a group setting that could make some people uncomfortable.
- Spring new rules on anyone without any notice and with no time to process.
- Change your mind at the last minute.

FROM NOW ON...

DISCOURTEOUS

BIG BRAIN *BONUS* TOOL

TIME PARACHUTES CREATE SOFT LANDINGS

TOOL

At times, an issue can seem like the most critical matter in the history of the universe. The perception by some will be that it demands immediate action.

In reality, not every decision must be made now. You can use a "Time Parachute" to give yourself a chance to jump out of an uncomfortable situation—and also give yourself time to consider an appropriate response. For example, it's hard to argue with a Time Parachute like, "Can I ponder that for a while?" or "Interesting...I need to understand more about this." Using a Time Parachute has a calming effect on all involved.

Sometimes, it can feel like a quick response is expected. If you receive a Little Brain message from someone and don't feel ready to respond from your Big Brain, use these time frames to keep yourself from falling into the Trap of replying from your Little Brain:

Take Your Time

- **Text:** Wait at least ten minutes—your message will be on the other person's phone forever.
- **Email:** Wait thirty minutes or more—your response will be on the other person's computer forever.
- **Voicemail:** Wait twenty-four hours or as long as it takes for you to calm down—it's your voice, and it will be recorded forever.
- **Social Media:** Wait as long as needed for your emotions to settle completely—everyone will have it forever, and it can be forwarded to the world.

Of course, we've all got to be nimble today. We have to keep up with the ever-increasing pace of the world around us. And we've always got to be at the top of our game. But hurrying and reacting in haste is not only counterproductive, it makes us look sloppy and, in the end, costs us more time.

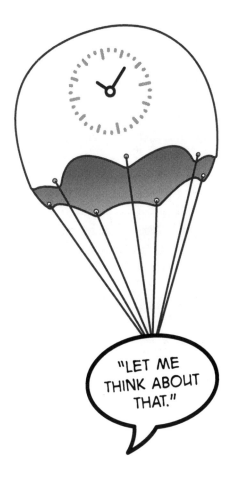

TIME TAKEAWAY

Time is often misunderstood as an adversary. Calendar management is the key to keeping time on your side.

- When people are under time pressure, their Little Brains can be easily activated.
- Communicate any major changes to routine or important news well in advance; it keeps people from overreacting.
- Avoid ambushing others with last-minute requests or new work that has to be done immediately.
- When you are feeling ambushed, use a Time Parachute to give yourself time to assess the situation.
- Before you push send, ask yourself, "Is this something I want everyone to read?"

"In the long run, we shape our
lives, and we shape ourselves.
The process never ends until we
die. And the choices we make are
ultimately our own responsibility."

—Eleanor Roosevelt, longest-serving
First Lady of the United States,
diplomat, and activist

CHAPTER 11

PRINCIPLE 5:
RESPONSIBILITY

THE LATE ARRIVAL

On a busy Friday morning, Fred, a rising star quickly moving up at a new startup in Silicon Valley, arrived very late for an important presentation. His supervisor, Stephanie, met him at the entrance to the team meeting.

"You're late," said Stephanie.

"Genius!" Fred said in a snide tone as he quickly walked by. "I guess that's why they made you the project manager!"

Stephanie couldn't believe her ears. Fred's Little Brain reaction awakened her Little Brain, which felt disrespected in front of everyone and jumped to get back at him.

In a voice loud enough to be overheard by the entire team, she exclaimed, "What the &@#! did you say? How dare you. You hotshot engineers think you can get away with anything!"

The project team gave each other the side-eye and watched closely to see how this moment would play out.

THE BIG BRAIN RESPONSE

Good thing for Fred that Stephanie's tone woke him up. Suddenly aware that his Little Brain had reacted badly and begun a dangerous encounter, his awareness quickly kicked in to help him instantly pivot from Little Brain to Big Brain.

"I'm so sorry, Stephanie," he said immediately and sincerely. "I really am. That was rude of me. It's no excuse, but I got into a car accident on my way here. Someone side-swiped me. When the police asked for my insurance card, I didn't have it with me, so I got a ticket for $720. Now I have to go to court to show proof, and I have to get my car fixed because the other guy didn't have insurance. Please forgive me."

This split-second Big Brain change of attitude transformed Stephanie's perspective on the encounter. "Fred," she said, much calmer now that she was responding from her Big Brain, "thanks for letting me know. Is the fine really that much?"

Carla, a coworker, chimed in, "Yes, but sometimes they'll waive it. I'll help you with the paperwork if you want."

Now sympathetic to Fred's predicament, Stephanie added, "Wow, Fred...that is a bad day. And Carla, thanks so much for offering to help out. So sorry it happened, and we're all glad you're okay. I apologize for my language and comment."

"No apology needed," Fred said. "I caused that reaction."

Stephanie smiled and looked at her watch. "Let's get the meeting started."

THE LITTLE BRAIN REACTION

Fueled by Fred's reckless outburst and Stephanie's reaction, the situation could have escalated to a level that would easily have been dangerous to Fred's career: insubordination, disrespecting a supervisor in front of others, missing important meetings...these are professional disasters that can be hard to recover from. It could have escalated well beyond what actually happened. Let's take a look.

"What the &@#! did you say?" Stephanie asked angrily.

The project team gave each other the side-eye and watched closely to see how this moment would play out.

Fred said, "Cut me a break, will you? I'm having a bad day."

"Bad day or not, Fred, I will not be spoken to that way," she said. "I know you think you're a hotshot, but make no mistake! I can get a dozen programmers here by noon to take your place."

"Just what I would expect from a heartless boss like you. I get into an accident that is not my fault, and you want to harass me even more—for being a little late? Really?"

The following week Fred found himself sipping coffee at his favorite coffee house, sitting with his laptop, looking for a job.

ELEMENTS OF RESPONSIBILITY

In the international best-selling book, *The Success Principles*, Jack Canfield with Janet Switzer, tell us there's only one person Responsible for the quality of the life you live on this earth...

and that person is *you*. When you realize that you—not your circumstances or other people—are responsible for your success (or lack of it), your life will dramatically shift:

> *When you accept that your actions (or inaction), your thoughts, and the words you say have tremendous sway over your results, then you will have taken the most important step of all toward a life of freedom, abundance, and fulfillment.*

How true is this when it comes to taking 100 percent responsibility for your success, but it's even truer when it comes to taking 100 percent responsibility for your communications.

CHOOSE TO ACCEPT RESPONSIBILITY

You've probably heard of the blame game: it has millions of participants but never any winners.

You know how it goes. Something goes wrong. Pretty soon, explanations are put forth about why it's someone else's mistake. Then the situation devolves into who is better at finger-pointing and denying responsibility.

The flip side of dishing out blame, on the other hand, is accepting responsibility. We will all slip up at some point and create a Little Brain moment. But by taking responsibility, you can easily guide the moment back to Big Brain territory. When you do, you'll strengthen your ability to improve your relationships and gain the respect of others.

It's a time to honor yourself more often (privately) and others more often (publicly) for the moments when you stepped up and did what was right, whether accepting responsibility or simply handling a task that no one else wanted to touch. You

PRINCIPLE 5: RESPONSIBILITY

will lead others by example. Nobody's perfect—your Big Brain accepts this, takes responsibility for mistakes, and knows that the best response is to be the bigger person.

WHAT YOU DON'T SAY...SAYS A LOT ABOUT YOU

Cicero, the Ancient Roman philosopher and statesman, put it another way: "Great is our admiration of the orator who speaks with fluency and discretion." We often have the urge to give our opinions and thoughts on various matters. But what you don't say—and when you don't say it—reveals a lot about you. Discretion is like gold. It is far more valuable when it is in short supply—and today, it seems in very short supply. Having the power of information and not using it, or knowing embarrassing but irrelevant facts about someone, must always be balanced against, "Is this the right place? Is this the right group to hear this? Does anyone ever really need to hear this?"

Little Brain's need for instant gratification is anxious to get everything out and get credit for being "in the know" no matter what the cost. Big Brain, by contrast, knows the value of discretion.

TOOLS AND TRAPS OF RESPONSIBILITY

Responsibility can be a tool for Big Brain thinkers. You might be thinking, *But isn't acting responsibly just a habit or something I do?* Hardly. In fact, it requires real effort to take the high road, be the bigger person, and take responsibility.

BIG BRAIN TOOL

"THAT'S ON ME"

TOOL

How do you steer clear of blaming others and instead take responsibility? Don't be afraid to accept responsibility for actions you've taken, words you've spoken, or decisions you've made.

We don't often hear, "It's my fault," or "That's on me."

When you quickly acknowledge your responsibility in making a misstep, you immediately begin to remedy its Legacy. The sooner you take ownership of your mistakes, the more respect you gain. Your response to those tricky moments will show others the way.

LEGACY REWARDS

HONORABLE

I TAKE FULL RESPONSIBILITY.

LITTLE BRAIN TRAP

TRAP

BLAME AND COMPLAIN

We've all heard those Little Brain blame phrases a hundred times: "It's not my fault." "They did it!" "The whole world is against me." "It's not my job."

When people hide from responsibility for decision-making or want to blame others for their decisions, it's an attempt to avoid responsibility for the outcome. This Trap often pops up when something goes wrong, and people are looking for someone to take the fall. However, ultimately, blaming is a distraction that does not work. Blaming or complaining excessively can instead identify you as part of the problem. It would be better to look for "what"—rather than "who"—went wrong. What needs to happen going forward?

WHINING

IT'S NOT MY FAULT, SOMEONE ELSE SCREWED UP.

BIG BRAIN LITTLE BRAIN

BIG BRAIN TOOL
EXPRESSED GRATITUDE

TOOL

Unexpressed gratitude is like a bucket of water sitting in the sun next to a flower. If the water is not poured onto the flower, the water will simply evaporate, and the flower will wither away. The opportunity—the moment—is lost. People and plants need to be nurtured. Why let the water evaporate instead of using it to bring out the best in the flower? In the same way, we often withhold appreciation we should ideally extend to others—either due to our limited time and focus or because we've simply made appreciation and recognition a low priority.

Instead of holding onto your silent appreciation, do your best to practice the Big Brain Tool of expressing gratitude.

You can always:

- Tell others what their efforts mean to you.
- Look for ways to give credit to others, especially in front of others.
- Seek opportunities to highlight your appreciation.

Giving small gifts or doing good deeds will be welcomed and have a long-term positive impact.

LEGACY REWARDS

APPRECIATIVE

THANK YOU, I'M SO GRATEFUL FOR YOUR HELP ON THIS. IT HAS MADE A DIFFERENCE...

TRAP

PROFESSIONAL POUTING

Pouting is the ultimate Trap of the pessimist and Little Brain. People caught in the Trap of pouting:

- Say to themselves, consciously or subconsciously, "I'm not happy, so nobody else should be happy."
- Act resentful when others get more attention or are more successful.
- Appear chronically annoyed and invent injustices to validate their distorted perception of reality.

Professional pouters can become more comfortable with being annoyed at the world than actually resolving their own problems or taking responsibility for their lives and choices.

RESENTFUL

NOBODY EVER THANKS ME...

NO EXPIRATION DATE ON APOLOGIES

TOOL

Remember the previous chapter on time? When a Little Brain "oops" moment occurs, and you've been insensitive, insulting, or rude, a quick apology can get the relationship back on track. But if there wasn't an opportunity for an apology in the moment—either the situation was highly charged or the person was suddenly unavailable to speak with you—there is still good news.

There's no expiration date on an apology.

We all say the wrong thing once in a while. We will all slip into Little Brain mode from time to time. But only the courageous among us take the time to apologize when it's appropriate.

Remember that perfection is unattainable, so don't hold yourself to an impossible standard. But that doesn't mean you have to settle for a lower standard when you recognize areas where you can improve. An apology—heartfelt and sincerely made—can go a long way toward repairing damage you may have consciously or subconsciously caused.

When you've said something wrong or just made a mistake, whether in words or deeds, do your best to apologize. Healing can start when a truly sincere apology has been given. Big Brain can always find a way to create a positive legacy. No matter how long it has been, there truly is no expiration date on a sincere apology. It's always the right time to apologize.

LEGACY REWARDS

SINCERE

I SCREWED UP LAST MONTH, AND I'M SORRY.

RESPONSIBILITY TAKEAWAY

Taking responsibility, apologizing, and expressing gratitude are all parts of Big Brain communication.

- Everyone makes mistakes once in a while. When it's your turn, take responsibility instead of trying to find someone to blame.
- Make a sincere apology when you need to. Don't let things fester.
- Show your gratitude and appreciation as often as possible. Unexpressed recognition is a missed opportunity.
- The more comfortable you are using these tools, the more comfortable your life will become.

"What lies in our power to do,
lies in our power not to do."

—Aristotle, Ancient Greek
philosopher and scientist

CHAPTER 12

PRINCIPLE 6:
POWER

THE POWER TO SEE BEYOND THE MOMENT

Jane stretched her aching shoulders and glanced at the clock: 10 p.m.

Jane's small graphics and design company was just beginning to make a splash in the industry. Known for its creativity, intelligent design choices, and ability to meet large demands on small time frames, the company was quickly developing a real buzz as the new player in town.

She and her team had just put the finishing touches on a new product campaign for a fast-growing energy drink company.

After eleven revisions throughout the day, she had finally received approval from Harley, the product manager of the beverage company and Jane's main point of contact. As her team began to pack up for the night, they were exhausted but satisfied by a job well done.

Jane called everyone into her office to enthusiastically note their accomplishments.

Suddenly, Jane's assistant burst into the room. "Harley is on the phone. He wants to talk to you *now*."

Jane motioned for everyone to hold back and picked up the receiver in the conference room. As soon as she heard Harley's fast-paced speech on the other end, she knew what he was about to say.

"Jane, I have a few more changes. I need three more additions and several changes done immediately—and by immediately, I mean in the next three hours. I have to get this out by 7 a.m. tomorrow."

Jane could feel the knots in her neck tighten.

Harley began listing his demands. Annoyed, Jane began taking a mental inventory of who was still available. Harley's suggestions were good, but Jane's entire team would have to scramble to meet his demands on time.

She didn't want to damage her firm's reputation in the marketplace because one client didn't respect their time. To assume that any changes could be made within such a short time frame was presumptuous at best.

Jane was brought back to the moment by Harley saying, "Can you do it? If you can't, I will find someone who can."

THE BIG BRAIN RESPONSE

Barely able to contain her annoyance, Jane jumped into Neutral and said, "Could you hold on for just a second?" in a tone so nice that Jane herself was surprised.

Harley didn't make the situation any better when he added, "Fine. Just make it fast. I will find another company if I have to."

Jane put Harley on hold and looked around at her group of designers who were milling around, waiting to see what she needed. She gave them the short list of Harley's demands and braced herself for their response.

"This guy is completely unreasonable!"

"Who does he think he is?!"

"That's it. I've had enough. That guy is such an #$@&*!%."

Jane felt that the design team's annoyance, long hours, exhaustion, and stress could easily allow her Little Brain reaction to take over and tell Harley no. She also knew she had three problems to deal with—a team that was overworked, a client whose time line could easily overwhelm them, and a third problem: payroll. She simply could not afford to lose a client. Jane decided to deal with Harley first.

Picking up the phone again, Jane took a breath into Neutral.

"Okay, Harley. Your suggestions are great. It will be tight to meet your deadline, but I think we can do it as long as we are on the same page and stay there."

Jane could hear the relief in Harley's voice as they went over specifics. At the end of the call, Harley said, "You guys are great. I know I'm asking a lot, but I really need it."

Hanging up, Jane turned to the team, who were still milling about the room.

"Look," Jane began, "I know we are all tired and want to move on. But we are in a deadline business—we all know that and this is the career we've chosen. But if you have to go, I will understand. Nothing will be held against you. I know it's late. For those who want to stay, we all need to work together if we're going to make this happen. Now, let's get going."

Despite their initial aggravation, Jane's team all agreed to stay. Together, they incorporated Harley's newest ideas into the campaign. Their new version took all night and was finished at 6 a.m., an hour before the deadline.

Ten minutes later, Harley called to thank everyone and commend them on a job well done. Jane went from team member to team member, thanking them each for all of their hard work and passing on Harley's appreciation. Relieved, many members of her team apologized for their reaction and commended Jane on her ability to keep her cool in a tough situation.

Jane's ability to understand the power she had in that moment was the key to getting the job done. When a powerful client is demanding, she understood the real power was to keep everyone focused on the job. Her concentrated actions strengthened her power within the industry. She began pulling in even more contracts from powerful clients, which, in turn, helped her grow her business. By not letting the pressure of the moment define her, she not only reinforced her ability to lead her team but also her position of leadership within the industry.

Two days later, Jane called to ask Harley for a face-to-face meeting at his office. There she explained that his "I will get someone else" comment—after signing off on the project just minutes before—was not only unprofessional but required an apology. Harley agreed. He apologized to Jane on the spot and offered to pay a higher rate for rushing the team and going back on his approval. She replied that, while she would accept that resolution, a handwritten note of appreciation to her team would actually bring the most value.

Jane's ability to see beyond the moment gave her power not only over the untenable situation but also power over her exhausted team, who were clearly in Little Brain mode. By not succumbing to reactionary Little Brain thinking herself, Jane saved the client account and created a major win for her growing company.

THE LITTLE BRAIN REACTION

It could have happened very differently, however...

If Jane had given in to impulse and told Harley that he was being unreasonable, she would have won the momentary accolades of her team but lost the opportunity to grow her business. The long-term impact on her company would have put their future in doubt.

ELEMENTS OF POWER

When you stay in Big Brain mode during any encounter, you give yourself power over the situation and maintain yourself as a powerful force for resolving problems and advancing the relationship. Engaging in Little Brain behavior, on the other hand, gives up this power to others who can (and probably will) make decisions and judgments based on your behavior.

POWER!

The desire for power is a primal human instinct, but this power doesn't have to be overpowering or negative. We've all experienced or heard about abuses of power but when you use power appropriately, it can keep people comfortable, make things run smoothly, and strengthen your Big Brain.

Little Brain finds power elusive. It strives for it, clutches for it, and when it's able to snatch it in tiny pieces, it is very protective and squirrels it away. Little Brain usually gets power through someone else or through position; it's not good at commanding power naturally. Little Brain holds on tight to what little power it has, often abuses it, and is always hungry for more.

Big Brain's relationship with power is quite different. Power comes easily to Big Brain because it isn't looking for it. Big Brain is most interested in a positive outcome for everyone involved, so it uses its power for the greater good, which coincidentally tends to bring it even more power. Big Brain gains its power by natural command and respect.

CHOOSE TO USE POWER WISELY

Bill Gates said, "As we look ahead into the next century, leaders will be those who empower others." Empowering others by supporting them, giving them room to be themselves, allowing them to make mistakes, and shepherding them when needed, will ultimately bring you the power to accomplish what you desire.

So often we think of power strictly in terms of who has the power and who doesn't. But we all have some level of power. Power is the most potent when it is shared. True power is never needing to show that you possess it.

POWER CAN EASILY WORK AGAINST YOU

One particularly destructive use of power is holding a grudge. Holding grudges against people ironically gives that person enormous power over you. Advice columnist Ann Landers once said that when you're holding a grudge against someone, you're allowing them to live rent-free in your head. When you hold grudges, you create a little strongbox in which you hang on to every minor injustice. At any time, you can pull one out and spring it on someone as "ammunition." You can use lots of little tricks to convince yourself that you have the right to settle a score with others. You tell yourself, "I can't let this go until I get them back." Punishing people makes your Little Brain feel powerful in that moment, but it also starts a vicious cycle of Little Brain activities. Ultimately, it gives your Little Brain the power and weakens your Big Brain. It leaves a Legacy of being unforgiving, vengeful, or begrudging.

Whether power is used positively or negatively, it will leave a strong Legacy.

NO DRIVER'S LICENSE FOR LITTLE BRAIN

The average weight of an automobile is a little over 4,000 pounds—a powerful force moving down the highway. Behind that much force, it's easy to feel safe with your reactions. But when you combine that weight with the speed in which a car can travel, you can see the enormous damage that can be done if these vehicles become extensions of Little Brain anger. That's what Olivia—in our story in Chapter Four—was thinking as she avoided the reckless freeway driver on her way to her son's graduation.

Knowing how Little Brain can take control of any moment clarifies why it is critical to ensure that it never gets behind the wheel. Road rage begins with a perceived slight. Intentional or unintentional, something happens between two drivers such that one believes the other is in the wrong. From there, the two parties begin a series of insults with hand gestures, or worse, moving across lanes. That can escalate the incident to a level where the cars become weapons—endangering themselves, but also others who are not even involved in the hostile exchange.

Getting cut off in traffic or having someone drive poorly is frustrating. No amount of frustration is worth the potential injury that road rage can produce. Don't let Little Brain get you into a road rage mistake. Always keep Big Brain in the driver's seat.

Little Brain also shows up quickly in the high-stakes challenge of acquiring a parking spot, especially when people are in a hurry. If you've ever been to a busy shopping center, you've seen plenty of examples of mini-battles for parking spaces. The battle has been going on since the first parking space was marked.

"It's mine!" people seem to say.

Big Brain will remind you that if someone "steals" your parking space, it's not worth a confrontation. The same time spent arguing will be the same as the amount of time spent parking a little further away. Be the one who lets it go. It's only a parking space.

> *"As we look ahead into the next century, leaders*
> *will be those who empower others."*
> —*Bill Gates*

TOOLS AND TRAPS OF POWER

Whether you maintain power in all situations—or give up your power to others through rage, negative assumptions, or other Little Brain behavior—is always your choice.

BIG BRAIN TOOL
EMPOWERING OTHERS

TOOL

As we learned from Jane's story, giving power to others to make the decision to stay or go gave the team a boost. Everyone appreciated having the power to leave, but all chose to stay.

Jane knew her power came from giving others the choice, even though she had the power to demand they stay.

Empowering others gives you strength. You are actually far more powerful in an encounter when you have the insight to allow a moment to play out without trying to wrestle for the win and allow others to have their moment. Big Brain encourages other Big Brains and is seen as a great mentor.

LEGACY REWARDS

TRUSTING

THANK YOU FOR GIVING US THE CHOICE.

TRAP

GIVING POWER AWAY

Giving away your power is not the answer. When you are naïve and fail to protect yourself, you can end up in situations you aren't prepared to handle. If you're easily persuaded by flattery and false compliments, or if your need to be liked is more powerful than your common sense, you can find yourself making Little Brain decisions on a regular basis. Little Brain can make you:

- Fearful of hurting someone's feelings or of being disliked to the extent you avoid all confrontation or even refuse to stand up for yourself.
- Ignore danger signs and allow others to push you into situations and decisions you regret.
- Believe that letting someone else always lead is easier than making a decision of your own.

To fail to engage due to fear hands control over to others.

FOOLISH

I DIDN'T WANT TO HAVE TO MAKE A DECISION.

BIG BRAIN TOOL
FORGIVENESS

TOOL

Gandhi said it so well: "The weak can never forgive. Forgiveness is an attribute of the strong." Carrying the problems of the past forward is like collecting big rocks in a backpack on the way up a mountain. Take a look at the rocks you've been carrying—whether someone else harmed you or you created a negative outcome for yourself—and start reframing those memories as lessons rather than injuries. Forgive others, but forgive yourself, too. You'll be released from the weight of those memories, and you'll move forward more prepared for the future. Start throwing rocks away and lighten your load.

LEGACY REWARDS

COMPASSIONATE

WE ALL MAKE MISTAKES... LET'S MOVE ON.

LITTLE BRAIN TRAP
THE PARTING SHOT

Always trying to get the last word in a conversation is a classic Little Brain Trap. You feel the need to be the last to speak because you believe the person who speaks last wins the moment. Trying to get the last word in, you might:

- Be unable to let a moment end on someone else's joke or clever comment.
- End the encounter with a cynical cliché.
- Frown or shrug your shoulders and walk away.

Little Brain fighting for the last word leaves a Legacy of needing attention and being insecure. Big Brain instead recognizes there's a larger moment at play and focuses its energy on the overall Legacy.

We've all seen the moment when somebody finishes a great conversation but just can't hold back that final snarky comment. It takes away from everything else they said and usually becomes all that's remembered.

SARCASTIC

WHATEVER...

BIG BRAIN *BONUS* TOOL
POWERFUL GOODBYE

TOOL

The farewell is the last chance you will have while still in the moment to leave a Big Brain Legacy. When you use the Powerful Goodbye, you actively seek ways to end an encounter on a positive note. Everyone will look forward to seeing you again. You might pair it with a Big Brain Goodbye, such as:

- "I appreciate our conversation."
- "Thanks for listening."
- "See you soon."

Even a simple "Thank you" can work wonders. Big Brain knows that leaving every moment with a smile creates a Legacy of friendliness, trust, and encouragement.

LEGACY REWARDS

CORDIAL

LOOKING FORWARD TO NEXT TIME.

POWER TAKEAWAY

When used properly, power can create wonderful moments in any relationship. Your power to affect the lives of others will have the longest Legacy of all.

- You look stronger when you share power.
- Seek ways to allow others to shine.
- Don't give away your power by holding a grudge.
- Forgiveness will release your burden and increase your personal power.
- Don't let Little Brain behind the wheel.
- Keep Big Brain in power by keeping Little Brain in check.

"I think self-awareness is probably
the most important thing
towards being a champion."

—Billie Jean King, Champion for
equality and winner of thirty-nine
Grand Slam tennis titles

CHAPTER 13

PRINCIPLE 7:
AWARENESS

IMPERFECT ENCOUNTER, PERFECT LEGACY

A moment etched in history. The story of Detroit Tigers' Pitcher Armando Galarraga. He was on his way to pitching a perfect game against the Cleveland Indians on June 2, 2010, only to have the umpire make a very bad call on the final out of the last inning. What the call should have been was obvious to the rest of the world and to Galarraga. The runner at first base was out, and it should have been a perfect game. A replay proved what everyone knew: the runner was out. But the umpire had called him safe, taking away one of the most prized achievements in all of baseball—the perfect game.

THE BIG BRAIN RESPONSE

Galarraga, though in total disbelief, did not overreact. He went directly into Neutral. He smiled, went back to the mound, and pitched the next batter out, ending the game as a one-hitter.

The enormity of the event set the media on fire. It seemed for a while that the entire sports world wanted revenge on the umpire who—once he saw the video himself—could not believe that he'd made such a bad call. But it was too late. Even though the umpire felt terrible, this was at a time when there was no official instant replay in baseball that would allow a change to the call. Nothing could be done. The airwaves were filled with people who wanted the decision reversed, and what they said about the umpire was down-right mean.

But in a game where foul language, physical outbursts, and bench-clearing brawls are not uncommon, Galarraga did not buy into the anger of others or the sadness at losing his spot in history. He did not join in the name-calling. He seemed to understand more than most that bad calls can happen in baseball, just as in life.

Immediately after the game, the umpire, James Joyce, asked Galarraga to come to the umpire's room. Joyce had been crying, and his body language spoke more than his words. Galarraga gave the umpire a heartfelt hug of forgiveness and said, "We are all human."

In the 130-year history of baseball, there had been only nineteen perfect games. At the most unexpected time, in a most difficult encounter, in one of the most emotional moments in all of baseball, Galarraga pitched a Big Brain response and secured himself a place in baseball history.

What was the Legacy of Galarraga's response? The next day, in front of thousands of cheering fans, Galarraga received a brand-new Corvette convertible from General Motors for the sportsmanship he exhibited. The Baseball Hall of Fame asked for his spikes and for the first base bag from the infamous play to place in its museum, along with the story of the moment. Instead of being on the bottom of a list of nineteen, Galarraga is at the top of a list of his own. But the Legacy of the story does not end there. Galarraga and Joyce became good friends and partnered to write a book about the experience. Galarraga won a perfect Legacy.

THE LITTLE BRAIN REACTION

If Galarraga was not Galarraga—if he had started screaming and jumping up and down—he would have had the whole stadium behind him. The media mob would have relished in his anger, and the vitriol towards the umpire would have been much worse. No car, no hall of fame, no new friendship.

ELEMENTS OF AWARENESS

There are some moments in life that we just know are too important to be handled with immaturity, acting out, or indulging in inappropriate behavior—in other words, Little Brain reactions. This knowledge is what we recognize as awareness.

KNOWS HIMSELF

Imagine if Galarraga's reaction had mirrored the rest of the sporting world's apoplectic outrage and their need to call the umpire names, kick up some dirt, and call on everyone to be on

Galarraga's side. The game would still have ended the same way, but Galarraga and everyone else could have gone on talk shows complaining about the unfair call. A few weeks would have passed, and the incident would have faded away behind new headlines, only to be brought up once in a while as an example of a bad call.

Thankfully, Galarraga's response in that moment is now a positive part of baseball history and is often cited as an example of what sportsmanship looks like. You never know when a moment will demand more from you than you had planned to give.

BE THERE

At Disney's theme parks, mirrors are posted in the backstage area near the exit to the guest area. This gives cast members one last chance to make sure that their uniforms or costumes are in place. The last thing they see before heading into the park is their own image.

As important as it is to maintain professional images at work, it's even more important that you have your mind in the right place—focused and aware of Big Brain and Little Brain encounters, moments, and legacies that are to come. If you don't have a mirror to look into as you leave the house, you may want to put up a reminder to stay in Big Brain mode, just to keep your awareness piqued. "Have a Big Brain Day" may sound a little corny, but focus is the key to awareness. Find a phrase that can remind you to stay aware—whatever works for you.

When you begin moments by saying to yourself, I've been thinking about this possibility, and I know what I want out of this encounter, you are anticipating. Preparing for positive communication, planning your desired Legacy even before the encounter begins (and remaining focused on it), or even being aware of potential traps that could arise allows you to approach every moment ready for whatever may happen. By anticipating how to best communicate your message and remain aware of what may get in the way, your Big Brain is ready for whatever may come.

Before you go into any encounter with anyone, always ask yourself what you want from the encounter. Don't let the Legacy occur by happenstance. Plan for it and positive moments are almost always assured.

> *Your Big Brain keeps a big view and is consciously working toward a Legacy of awareness.*

BIG BRAIN PUSH-UPS

As an exercise, think about last week. Look at your calendar, your emails, and your texts. Identify the moments that stick out in your mind, whether they were positive or negative. If you aren't happy with how you handled some of those moments, what could you have done differently? Do you need to do any follow-up damage control?

Now think about next week. Look at your calendar. How can you best ensure that your upcoming moments will turn into Big Brain legacies? Which moments are likely to start or possibly end in Little Brain legacies, given the people you might meet or what you'll be doing or talking about? What can you anticipate to help keep Little Brain in check?

BIG VIEW, LITTLE VIEW

Keeping a satellite view of situational awareness in any given moment allows you to see everything in the atmosphere around you. Don't get caught in the trap of tunnel vision. As a result, you fail to recognize the Influences you may be under in the moment. Tunnel vision keeps you oblivious to who might be in the room or the potential greater consequences of that moment.

Allowing your Big Brain to bring a satellite view lets you recognize the Influences of the moment before you respond. Your Big Brain keeps a big view, and is consciously working towards a Legacy of awareness, perspective, and trustworthy responses.

If a moment begins with someone in Little Brain mode, remind yourself that you might have an activated person in front of you, but you are still in control of your reaction to the moment. Even though the conversation may not be starting out in a friendly way, your Big Brain sees the bigger picture and can steer it in a more positive direction—and toward your positive Legacy.

TOOLS AND TRAPS OF AWARENESS

While many people on the other side of an encounter aren't focused on the outcome (as you are), by exercising awareness in that moment, you can make all the difference between a favorable outcome and a poor Legacy.

EXITS AND ENTRANCES

TOOL

You may not have control over all the events that come your way every day, but there are at least four minutes throughout the day that repeat themselves on a regular basis—putting you in the same environment, the same scenario, and the same opportunity for awareness. If you focus on these few minutes, they can help start and end your day with a positive legacy.

1. The Closing Minute at Home

Leaving for work or school in the morning can be a very rushed moment. Assembling last-minute items and feeling the pressure to get out the door on time creates an environment that is not good for serious discussions about anything. Let the last-minute walking out the door from the house be a moment of support, not surprise. Everyone will leave for the day remembering your last smile and well-wishing.

BYE, SEE YOU LATER.

2. The Opening Minute at Work/School

Walking through the door at work sets the tone for the entire day. Big Brain takes the time to say "Hello" and greet others, whereas Little Brain tends to walk by people without greeting them—sending a message that it really doesn't want to be bothered. To start out in Big Brain at the office, take this minute to acknowledge others, and then get on with the business of the day. At the same time, when you see people walking into work, Big Brain recognizes this isn't the best time to pile on tasks that need to be done or messages that have to be answered quickly. Give them a minute to get settled before engaging.

GOOD MORNING...

CONTINUED...

BIG BRAIN TOOL *(CONTINUED)*

3. The Closing Minute at Work/School

Take a moment when people are leaving to finish on an upbeat note and send them home thinking positive thoughts—especially on weekends. Pressing people at the end of the day or week for important answers can activate their Little Brain. It creates an unnecessary time pressure regarding issues that could have been dealt with earlier or could wait until the next business day. Focus on the good of the day, and extend well-wishes for their journey home.

> GOODBYE, SEE YOU TOMORROW.

4. The Opening Minute at Home

The minute people walk in the door from their day at work, school, or daily tasks may not be the best time to jump into the items that have been on your mind all day. Give yourself and others the first minute to set things down and transition to the home environment, using that first minute to release the day, reconnect, and recognize the opening of the evening at home. Try changing your shirt or top as a powerful metaphor that the day is behind you.

> HELLO! IT'S NICE TO BE HOME...

LITTLE BRAIN TRAP

TAKING IT PERSONALLY

TRAP

When you fall into the Trap of getting personally offended over the little things people say and do, you believe that others are always attacking you. You look for anything at all that you can be sensitive about, then project it onto the moment. As a result, you:

- Look for the negative in the comments made.
- Focus on self-pity, assuming, "They did this on purpose."
- Begin to plan how to get back at them.
- Ensure a negative legacy.

IMMATURE

THAT WAS ON PURPOSE BECAUSE THEY DON'T LIKE ME.

BIG BRAIN TOOL
TUNE INTO OTHERS

TOOL

Rather than making snap judgments about people, you can take the position that everyone has the right to be heard and understood. By staying open-minded, you listen to all sides, even if you disagree. Ultimately, by welcoming others' views and comments, you not only gain more insight into how to handle them in the future, you better understand them, their Influences, and their Activators.

Big Brain listens to others carefully. If it hears something that may be inappropriate, insensitive, or even insulting, it refuses to become offended and react in the moment. It understands, "This moment may have nothing to do with me." Through this heightened awareness, you can recognize that even when someone directs a harsh jab at you, that person is probably under the influence of something else in his or her life. It does not excuse the comment but rather puts it in perspective to deal with at the appropriate time and in an appropriate way.

When you tune into others, you're able to:

- Understand the viewpoints of others. While you may not accept them, they will feel heard.
- Hear what others are most concerned about.
- Listen to the tone of others to indicate if they are in Big Brain or Little Brain.
- See beyond the moment and give others time to gain perspective.

LEGACY REWARDS

INSIGHTFUL

I CAN HEAR THAT YOU ARE FRUSTRATED... IS THERE ANYTHING I CAN DO TO HELP?

LITTLE BRAIN TRAP

TRAP

ASSUMING THE NEGATIVE

When you assume the negative, those sour feelings can be difficult to shake, even when the assumptions are proved wrong. Maybe you scripted a negative outcome in advance, played out the encounter before it ever occurred, and now feel guarded. Sometimes, the Little Brain engages in self-imposed ignorance by wanting only enough information to validate its negative feelings and beliefs and prove its script was right.

Assuming the negative prevents you from hearing all sides because they might make you uncomfortable. After all, how could you be wrong? These negative scripts from the Little Brain will make you feel pessimistic about all kinds of encounters and can even ruin some moments. It's easy to judge people when you don't know the whole story. We assume things that may not be true but easily fit and reinforce our presupposed views. Assuming the negative creates even more negative energy and is a major Trap.

GLOOMY

THEY'RE DOING THAT BECAUSE THEY DON'T CARE.

BIG BRAIN *BONUS* TOOL
DAILY AWARENESS CHECKUP

TOOL

Remember how to check in on your Circle of Influences from Chapter Two? How is your Me today? Is it a strong Me or a weak Me? Look at your own Circle of Influences and try to identify any Influences present or acting on you today. **Are there any minor or major Influences affecting your Me?** Are any Influences in Big Brain or Little Brain mode?

Forming a daily habit of self-awareness can help strengthen your understanding of yourself. You'll get to know your Activators, recognize your biggest Influences, and become more aware of what boosts your Big Brain. Soon, you'll also begin to recognize how other peoples' Big Brain and Little Brain might be influenced, so you can respond accordingly. You'll be able to recognize if one of the Influences in their circle is having an impact on the moment.

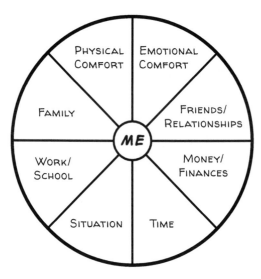

Your Circle of Influences

CONTINUED...

BIG BRAIN TOOL (CONTINUED)

To help you gain self-awareness, check in with yourself daily to understand which mode each of your Influences is in today. You can even create a little chart like this one to help you with this Daily Awareness Checkup.

Influence	in Big Brain mode	in Little Brain mode
Emotional Comfort	☐	■
Physical Comfort	☐	■
Family	☐	■
Friends/Relationship	☐	■
Money/Financial	☐	■
Work/School	☐	■
Time	☐	■
Situation	☐	■

LEGACY REWARDS

MINDFUL

In the end, awareness of others and recognizing what's good in the world not only leads to better communications, it leads to better health and happiness, too. There are so many examples that prove this to be true. I've already mentioned Dr. Henry Lodge's book, *Younger Next Year*. In it, he emphasizes that there is a "real premium on having positive emotions." In fact, cognitive therapy, says Dr. Lodge—the practice of shifting one's thoughts to more positive, helpful, and goal-oriented beliefs— "is as effective as medication in treating depression, and with a lower relapse rate." Wow! Interacting with others in a more positive, friendly, and less combative way can alleviate one of the most common ailments of modern society.

In addition, Dr. Lodge goes on to say that the connection we have with others—that positive emotional tie that our limbic brain works nonstop to form—can bring health, healing, and meaning to our lives.

Be aware. Connect positively with others. And watch your life change for the better.

AWARENESS TAKEAWAY

When you are aware, you have the freedom to choose the Legacy of the moment.

- Tune into whomever you are with and truly listen to what they are speaking about.
- Keep the four opening and closing minutes, at home and at work, focused and positive.
- Don't fall into the trap of assuming the negative.
- Being aware of who is in the room (and who they will talk to) allows you to keep your comments in perspective.
- Anticipate and identify the Influences involved in the encounter.
- Keep your Legacy as your guide for every encounter.

"Kind words can be short and easy to speak, but their echoes are truly endless."

—Mother Teresa, Saint Teresa of Calcutta, Founder of Missionaries of Charity

CHAPTER 14

YOUR **LEGACY**

THE LEGACY OF YOUR MOMENTS

The impact of a moment can be felt long after the moment has passed. There is a ripple effect to the moment. Its impressions or consequences leave a ripple effect that will layer and combine into your Legacy. It's how you will be remembered. The Legacy of each moment, positive or negative, adds to your reputation.

Big Brain understands this.

Little Brain isn't concerned with Legacy. It impulsively makes choices that can create damaging moments and messes to clean up.

Big Brain, on the other hand, actively seeks to shape its Legacy by creating positive moments. It knows that when people like and enjoy your company, they look forward to seeing you, they like being in a relationship with you, and they like working with you. They tell their friends how wonderful you are. You begin to build trust and friendship, and your relationships grow stronger and happier.

So many moments can pass by quickly in our everyday lives. How many times are we truly engaged in the conversation, aware of its impact and our choices? How many times are we absent-mindedly filling the silence between exchanges? The more conscious we are of our Legacy and our active part in creating it moment by moment, the more effectively we communicate.

HOW TO LIGHTEN YOUR BAGGAGE

Little Brain legacies can be permanent unless you take steps to remove them from your baggage. You can do this by identifying situations where you might have left behind undesired legacies and seek ways to undo them. You may need to offer an apology that's long overdue, fulfill a forgotten promise, or do something as simple as making a phone call someone has been waiting to hear. Just like apologies, there is no expiration date on tending to your Legacy. The choices to lighten your baggage are always available to you.

BIG BRAIN FINISHING TOUCHES

When we communicate from our Big Brain, our Legacy continues a healthy, positive ripple effect. Here are some Big Brain finishing touches you can use to make sure your moments end with a Big Brain Legacy:

- **End the moment positively.** Make sure that the final comment from you is always positive, warm, forgiving, empathetic, rational. Often, it's paired with a smile.

- **Follow up with a thank you.** Send a card, text, or email to recap the good time you had.

- **If needed, clarify.** Send a note to correct any possible misunderstandings that might have come up. Often questions will arise long after the moment is over. Follow through and make sure they're answered. Take time to review the moment to make sure that you didn't miss anything.

- **Apologize as soon as possible.** If a moment has ended and you realize that you owe an apology for something you said or did or something you forgot to say or do, don't waste time. The faster the apology, the faster the healing.

- **Forgive.** If someone offers you an apology after a moment has ended, acknowledge the apology as soon as you're ready. Even forgiveness needs processing time, so proceed at your own pace. Keep this in mind when you're apologizing to others, as well. Don't assume that just because you've apologized, the other person is ready just yet. Give them time.

It's easy to imagine how the Little Brain might have handled each of these finishing touches: purposely ending the moment negatively, failing to follow through, leaving things unclear, never apologizing, or holding on to grudges from long ago. Don't let Little Brain be the Legacy of a moment.

THINK LEGACY, THINK RIPPLE EFFECT

A moment can create, improve, worsen, or destroy a relationship, whether that relationship is long-standing or brand new. As we've seen throughout this book, it comes back to choice. Every moment is an opportunity not just for a beneficial or wounding encounter, but to choose that Legacy for yourself.

BEGIN

WHAT IS IMPORTANT NOW IS
WHAT YOU CHOOSE TO SAY NEXT

Every relationship is built on trust. The essence of the Big Brain Legacy is an increase in trust. From the first time we meet someone, that trust continues to build up or can be diminished with every encounter.

Of course, most people in our lives we've known for weeks, months, or years, and the first impression is long gone. However, your relationship now continues on with a series of last impressions. These impressions ultimately deserve equal or greater thought than the first.

In any encounter you have with someone, the most recent exchange sets the last impression. The last email you sent, the last text you pushed out, the last voice mail you left, the last tweet expressed, the last Instagram post, or the last comment you made in a face-to-face conversation...they all add to the last impression you are leaving with people. So when you are sending any form of communication, take a moment to realize the importance of what you are saying and how long it will endure. A good last impression is a powerful addition to your Legacy.

In any moment, shifting into Neutral and accessing your Big Brain's response is always available to you. As soon as Big Brain starts to take over, Little Brain immediately loses power, and you're on your way to a Big Brain Legacy. Your Neutral Word is your new best friend.

As these pages bring our encounter to a close, many new encounters are about to open for you. In the time it has taken to read this book, you have already become a better communicator. You have learned how to make the most of the moments in front of you. Before you know it, your Big Brain will be at the helm of each and every conversation in each and every moment—at home, at work, in life, and for the rest of your tomorrows.

Keep practicing Big Brain. Win the moments. Get into Neutral, and remember:

You have a choice.

REWARDS AND BAGGAGE

Now that you have learned how to look at every encounter differently, you are more aware of the benefits and consequences that play out in every conversation. You have learned how to make the most of every moment.

On the following pages, you will find a recap of the Legacy rewards and Legacy baggage. Keep them close so they can remind you of the benefits of keeping Big Brain in control and keeping Little Brain away.

BIG BRAIN LEGACY WORDS

These Legacy reward words are how others remember you and the encounters they have had with you. Take a look at the list and keep it close.

Everyone has Big Brain rewards, and when we put all of those Legacy moments together, we begin to see the big picture of how these legacies add up.

As you begin to choose Big Brain responses more often, your account expands. Your reputation improves.

You may have different Legacy rewards with different people, and you may even have some Legacy rewards and Legacy baggage with the same person.

Take a look at the different people in your life as you review the Legacy rewards and Legacy baggage words on the following pages. If you find you have baggage with anyone, you can learn how to remove that baggage by following the steps outlined in the "Lighten Your Baggage" section coming up.

BIG BRAIN LEGACY WORDS

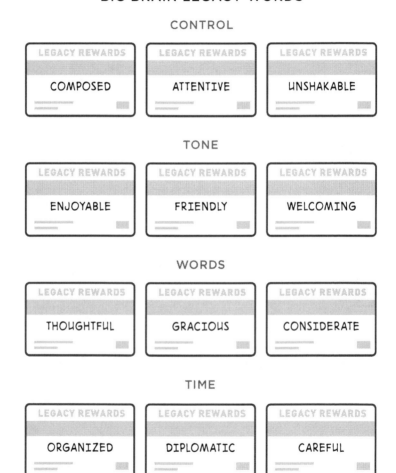

CONTROL

LEGACY REWARDS	LEGACY REWARDS	LEGACY REWARDS
COMPOSED	ATTENTIVE	UNSHAKABLE

TONE

LEGACY REWARDS	LEGACY REWARDS	LEGACY REWARDS
ENJOYABLE	FRIENDLY	WELCOMING

WORDS

LEGACY REWARDS	LEGACY REWARDS	LEGACY REWARDS
THOUGHTFUL	GRACIOUS	CONSIDERATE

TIME

LEGACY REWARDS	LEGACY REWARDS	LEGACY REWARDS
ORGANIZED	DIPLOMATIC	CAREFUL

RESPONSIBILITY

LEGACY REWARDS
HONORABLE

LEGACY REWARDS
APPRECIATIVE

LEGACY REWARDS
SINCERE

POWER

LEGACY REWARDS
TRUSTING

LEGACY REWARDS
COMPASSIONATE

LEGACY REWARDS
CORDIAL

AWARENESS

LEGACY REWARDS
INSIGHTFUL

LEGACY REWARDS
PRESENT

LEGACY REWARDS
MINDFUL

LITTLE BRAIN
BAGGAGE WORDS

Now let's look at all the potential Little Brain baggage that could have been packed away. In your Little Brain baggage, you could be lugging around a reputation filled with some of these baggage words without realizing it.

The good news is that with any Little Brain baggage you find, you have a chance to remove the baggage and replace it with a Big Brain reward by using the tools you have now learned in this book.

LIGHTEN YOUR BAGGAGE

We all have Little Brain moments that can create baggage. However, how long that baggage lasts is up to us.

To lighten your load, seek out opportunity conversations. The next time you encounter a person that you may have some baggage with, you might choose to offer an overdue apology or a clarification from a previous encounter. Or you might simply demonstrate your use of a Big Brain tool instead of falling into a Little Brain trap so that this new moment can move some baggage out and create a new rewards Legacy.

LITTLE BRAIN BAGGAGE WORDS

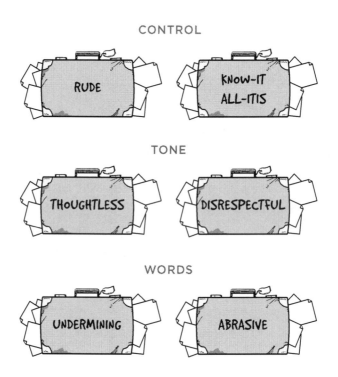

CONTROL

RUDE

KNOW-IT ALL-ITIS

TONE

THOUGHTLESS

DISRESPECTFUL

WORDS

UNDERMINING

ABRASIVE

TIME

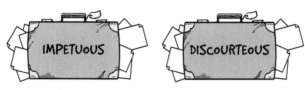

RESPONSIBILITY

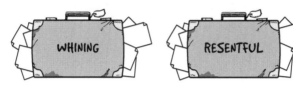

POWER

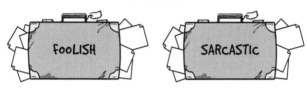

AWARENESS

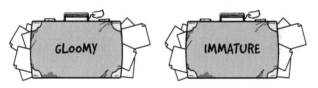

HAVE A BIG BRAIN DAY!

Get to Neutral.
Don't let Little Brain do the talking.
Keep your Big Brain in Control.

The Tone is the Message.
Choose the correct Tone.

Good Gossip works.
Choose the correct Words.

Keep Time on your side.
Choose the right Time.

Our choices, our Responsibility.
Express gratitude.

Use Power wisely.
Empower others.

Stay Aware of the Legacy.
The ripple effect will have a lasting impact.

AFTERWORD

Dear Reader,

You are now ready to begin a new chapter in your life—a chapter where you are in control of your responses and know how to deal with the ways others may be reacting or overreacting.

I would love to continue the conversation with you. Tell me about your Big Brain moments and your Little Brain moments. I would also love to hear about your Big Brain and Little Brain observations in life. Reach out any time at *Kevin@bigbrainlittle brain.com*, or visit me at *bigbrainlittlebrain.com* to see any updates.

And thank you—for sharing your time with me and for your curiosity about the internal forces of communication at play in each of us. By being aware of our own communication, and bringing more and more moments into Big Brain, we each inspire a more thoughtful, kind, and generous world.

May all your moments be Big.

Sincerely,
Kevin Thomas McCarney
Kevin@bigbrainlittlebrain.com